To Elkie my dearest friend and sister, also Bobby my native american I found you So blessed I found You. God sent you to Gary's Myself. You know we /we and adare are mixed family Luv Conde's Gary

The
Greatest Sound
on Earth

To Sylvia
and Ruth

Myron Richards
5/3/06

Author's Orchestra, 1910

The
Greatest Sound on Earth
or
Eine Kleine Alte Fahrt Mit Orchester

By Myron Richards

Illustrations by
Mark Jeffries

Perry Publishing
5788 Lene'a Drive NW
Bremerton, WA 98312

ISBN: 0-9622337-4-9
Library of Congress Catalog Card Number: 94-66243

Dedication

I dedicate this book to all the musicians with whom I worked over the active years of my professional career. You taught me how to make music, not just musical tones. You taught me the value of complete dedication to an art that can change the world for the listener, from a place of despair to a place of hope.

The symphony orchestra is truly the universal musical instrument and anyone who has had the privilege of making music as part of this instrument has been touched with a feeling for an eternal spirit far beyond our feeble understanding. My teachers have been legion. You tried to teach me everything you knew, but I still have much to learn.

I pay special tribute to Alvin Schardt, one of the greatest horn players who ever lived. Fate let me follow in his footsteps. It was apparent to all that no one could ever take his place.

M.R.

Programme of Contents
with
Annotations

Illustrations

Prelude

This literary effort is an attempt to share my thoughts, biases, experiences, feelings, and a few facts about the symphonic orchestra, the most highly developed musical grouping in the western world. I spent many years as an instrumentalist in a symphony orchestra, as well as doing pit work for ballet, opera, Broadway musicals, and in stage bands with visiting pop musicians, etc. All of what follows has been dredged up from my own imperfect memory with minimal reference to occasional books (unspecified) for a date or two. I promise that there will be inaccuracies, misinformation, opinions that no one has ever agreed with, and some downright lies. If you become too disturbed at what follows, then I apologize and look forward to reading the book that you write in order to set the record straight.

Included are: a made-up history of the development of the orchestra, a chapter about acoustics, a section on the kinds of people who usually are attracted to each different type of instrument, insider musician stories, a true story about a particular unnamed orchestra, a section about conductors, other musical trivia, plus some other information that may or may not be germane to the topic.

Chapter 1

A Waltz Through Orchestral History In Four/Four Time

Man has performed in groups for many activities since prehistoric times. The first group activities were probably for mutual protection and hunting. Man found that there was a secondary advantage to group activity: a sense of well being and self worth not as easily experienced when acting alone. Our culture has many examples of worthwhile group interaction including fraternal lodges, legislative bodies, design teams, barn raisings, quilting bees, team sports, etc. Man has also grouped together for fun activities since before recorded history, including games, rituals, dance, drama, and music. All of these have functions apart from food gathering, mutual protection, and shelter. Arguments can be initiated about the relative importance to the human spirit of actions not necessary to sustain life. Nevertheless, these activities are an on-going part of the universal cultural experience.

Music is one of the inexplicable behaviors of man. Why should the voice be made to function in non-speech sounds that use language, pitch, and rhythm that obscures and enhances meaning at the same time? Why did man add the use of voice imitators in the form of musical instruments which further obscure communication and why do groups of these instruments in various combinations retain great popularity?

Listeners to musical group presentations must receive positive reinforcement because a high percentage repeat the experience when the opportunity is available. The performers must also have positive reinforcement from the experience since many spend the rest of their lives performing in groups once they have tried it. For many people, experiencing the satisfaction of group participation in a musical endeavor can be so exhilarating that it becomes addictive.

Over the centuries certain patterns of musical groups seemed to predominate in Western European music. For many years groups most often were made up from the same families: all brass, all viols, etc. As violins replaced other stringed instruments and the science of musical harmony developed into the use of the interval of a third in vertical structure, the so-called string quartet became more or less standardized using two violins, one viola, and a violoncello. This grouping allowed three note chords to sound with a melody superimposed or other more complicated harmonic effects. From time to time other instruments were added to this basic instrumentation. Different instrumental combinations appeared until finally the basic orchestra had developed into a unit comprising the string quartet with several players on each part, plus a few woodwinds, an occasional brass player, and even a drum. The symphonic orchestra was just around the corner.

The modern orchestra appeared in the early seventeenth century to accompany opera. Perhaps if the piano had been invented by then the orchestra never would have come about, as the harpsichord, the predominant keyboard instrument then in use, was too soft to accompany any group singing on stage. The orchestra composers seem to start with Claudio Monteverde (1568-1643) who was the first to use the string quartet as the foundation of the orchestra. Then Allesandro Scarlatti (born 1659) used the quartet with oboes and flutes. Handel (1658-1759) used most of the present day orchestral instruments, except the clarinet, but assigned them in greater numbers on the same parts as the strings do today. Haydn's first symphony, written in 1759, was scored for first and second violins, violas and basses, two oboes and two horns. Note the absence of violoncelli which were added for his next symphony. (This may only reflect who was available for the occasion of the performance.) Mozart (1756-1791) added the clarinets so that the orchestra was complete as it is today, except for instruments added for special effects.

I suppose that the change to putting the orchestra on stage to entertain came from the pit orchestra playing the overture and other incidental music during the opera. I further suppose that the overture was an invention born of desperation when a singer was late arriving at the theater, or some other back stage calamity made it impossible to start at the expected time. The conductor was sent out front because the audience was getting restless at the delay. After acknowledging the scattered applause at his appearance, he then had to whisper enough instructions to the orchestra so that they could play a tune together to quiet the crowd. I would guess that the brass players never did find the right place to start, which only made the impromptu overture sound different later on in the evening when heard in its proper place. Anyhow, the orchestra finally got to sit up on the stage and entertain without help from the singers. Now they were compelled to dress up a bit and quit wiping their noses on their sleeves. Composers now began writing pieces just for the orchestra. The repertoire from this point consisted of opera overtures, a few dance tunes, maybe a drinking song, and whatever someone in the viola section felt like arranging from folk tunes.

The first problem the orchestra composers had was in what form to write, and what to call this new kind of writing. Most of them, being unimaginative fellows, just borrowed the sonata form invented by Haydn and named it "symphony". It probably is unfair to mention that symphony is an old name for a hurdy-gurdy but I'll mention it anyway.

By the time Beethoven came on the scene in the late 1790's, the instruments of the orchestra were more or less standardized. They are listed in order of appearance in the orchestral score which is the music the conductor refers to in rehearsal and sometimes turns pages of during the concert.

Flutes a pair (sometimes three)
Oboes a pair
Clarinets a pair
Bassoons a pair
Horns two pair (French horns to laymen)
Trumpets a pair
Trombones a pair (sometimes)
Tympani
Violin I
Violin II
Viola
Violoncello
Contrabass

The string parts are played by any number from four and beyond on each part. Other instruments added at various times include, but are not limited to, the following:

Piccolo
Alto flute
English Horn (big oboe)
Eb Soprano clarinet (Piccolo clarinet or epher)
Bass clarinet
Saxophones (soprano, alto and tenor)
More horns, up to eight and beyond
More trumpets, up to four
Bass trombone
Tuba
Harp
Snare drum
Bass drum
Other percussion (piano, mallet instruments
     and all manner of noisemakers up to and
     including cannon)

Thus we end up with a formidable array of musical instruments numbering one hundred, more or less, each one manipulated by a human being who probably spent more hours mastering the beast than your average brain surgeon spent practicing with his tools before hanging out a shingle after his audition. Why does anyone aspire to become a member of this elite group? As I mentioned previously, the intense concentration necessary in this group activity creates a feeling of joy which is almost euphoric at times, that once experienced becomes addictive.

Prediction is always difficult, especially with regard to the future, but I herewith share my thoughts about the ultimate destiny of the symphonic orchestra.

As I write (1994) there seems to be no shortage of well-trained, talented, and ambitious musicians on all instruments so that the orchestra seats can be filled as present people retire. In fact, I suspect that there are more players graduating from the top music schools than can possibly find employment.

One reason for this is that many fine orchestras around the country are finding it harder each year to find ways to pay off their deficits, and some have had to disband. (What's the difference between an orchestra and a band? In an orchestra the band sits in back! Oh, well.)

The electronic industry has already had a tremendous effect on the orchestra with recording techniques constantly improving. In a later chapter I will write about the difficulties encountered when first attempts were made to record the symphony orchestra mechanically. Now, I am told, recording engineers can even erase incorrect notes that may otherwise prohibit a perfect performance on record. It even seems to me, as I listen to some recordings, that the engineer has replaced the conductor in deciding which voices in the orchestra should predominate.

The year 'round, full-time employed symphony orchestra musician may become scarce in the years to come as orchestras continue to have funding problems, but I believe that amateur orchestras of high caliber will increase in number as men and women look for ways to enjoy the huge amount of symphonic literature at first hand.

Stuart Chase in his book, *Men And Machines*, writing about the industrial revolution notes that:

> "*The symphony orchestra made its bow into the world arm-in-arm with the first power-driven factories. It flourished and grew strong along with looms, locomotives, and milling machines. As I sit in the gallery at Carnegie Hall with half-closed eyes, watching the uniform flash of silver bows over white shirt fronts, the answer to this riddle drifts into focus. What is an orchestra but a cunningly articulated, and thoroughly standardized, factory of sound? Then as I sample the waves which reach my ears, and compare them to the currents from a rolling mill ~ the answer drifts out again. Perhaps music was the spar which saved the race from drowning through all those dreadful early years.*"

This may very well be significant of something, but on the other hand, maybe not.

Orchestra of the Future

Chapter II

Over The Fiddles
And Through The Woodwinds
To All Of The Brass We Blow

This chapter is an exploration of the personality of the professional symphony orchestra musician. The following generalities are the result of my own experiences in several different orchestras. The instruments exhibit personality that is recognized by the listener and so it seems reasonable that the musician's character, life style, and general personality will have at least some relationship to the chosen instrument.

The orchestral instruments all come under the broad categories of strings, woodwinds, brass, and percussion. A few musicians become professionally proficient on instruments of more than one of these categories but this is rather rare. Most musicians start learning an instrument in childhood and stay with the same one the rest of their lives. Many times logical thinking has little to do with that first choice. The reasons for making choices might include: Uncle Fred has a trombone not presently in use, mother knows someone who teaches violin, father always wanted to play the clarinet but never had the opportunity, or the child wants to play the trumpet because his best friend does.

The real unanswered question is, does the student go on to be a successful artist because of a happy choice that matches the personality or, does playing a particular instrument affect the development of the individual's thought processes so that certain personality traits are enhanced? You won't find an answer from me!

One orchestral organizational fact that must be explained before proceeding is that every instrument section has two classes of people: Chiefs and Indians. The Chiefs are variously called first chair players, section leaders, principal or soloists depending on local custom, clout, contract negotiations, etc. Those who are section leaders have personality traits not present in those who are not section leaders unless the particular Indian is a young ambitious squaw or brave. Section leaders are paid at a higher level than the others and they usually have additional responsibilities.

Their first justification for additional pay is that they perform the part in which the composer traditionally has written all solo passages for their instrument. This means that the first chair player is the only one on his instrument who the audience can identify to praise or blame for the sounds of that individual instrument. Occasionally section leaders may have to give direction in certain ways to all the others who perform on the same instrument. Others in the section may have to take advice from the section leader which may be distasteful or unnecessary.

The section members who are not first chair performers generally have an easier life for several reasons. If they are string instrumentalists, no one will ever hear a note that they play for the rest of their lives unless they are extremely inept or very unlucky. Section members can have a lot of fun by playing all the solos backstage before the concert that their section leader must perform that night. This is considered very bad manners but an ambitious musician who aspires to that first chair position will do anything that might throw a psychological curve to his not-too-well-respected colleague. The ultimate irony of this scenario is that after the first chair performer's contract has been declared open, because of obvious inability to conquer the nervous quavers brought on by one of his own musical partner's activities, the conductor will declare that there is no local performer of the high caliber required in this important post, but he knows of a player from the last orchestra which he conducted who can be persuaded, for more money of course, to come and fill the spot. All conductors subscribe to the dictum that an expert is someone from out of town. The conductor will, of course, be unable to detect that which is obvious to every member of the orchestra (including the drummer whose hearing has been permanently impaired by long hours spent in the center of cacophony otherwise known as the battery), the new section leader is not only no improvement, he is barely competent!

Before proceeding to the individual instrumentalists, a few remarks may be worthwhile about the characteristics of the various instruments.

Referring to an earlier statement, musical instruments are basically imitations of the human singing voice. Thus all wind instruments, because they use the breath to produce the sounds, should produce the most natural and realistic music. An examination of the way other instruments operate sustains the idea. This does not mean that other instruments are less valid, only that for them to produce music requires a certain amount of illusion which increases the difficulty in performance. Dragging a dead horse's tail across some former cat's intestinal membranes produces a different type of vibratory tonal delight than that emanating from the vocal chords of a skilled singing voice. Striking a tightly stretched string with a hammer activated by a complicated lever system produces a tone extremely loud and harsh which then dies away, totally unlike even the sound produced by an unskilled singer.

One other wind instrument, though not a regular orchestral member, needs to be mentioned. The pipe organ uses moving air to produce its sounds, but its air supply is mechanically produced and so there is never a gap for inhaling. This removes the natural human element and so most performers fail to produce believable music from it.

These basic differences between strings and winds affect the people who can find satisfaction on one or the other. Beginning wind instrumentalists can very quickly produce an acceptable musical tone on their instrument, but even the great concert violinists sounded dreadful when they first started. Some explanation involving personal character is needed to explain why a string player would persevere in the study of an instrument without satisfactory feedback. I offer three possible reasons.

> 1. The person is so insensitive that the horrible nature of the result goes unnoticed.
> 2. The student has heard good playing and enjoys the challenge of hard work leading to improvement.
> 3. Parental pressure demands that the investment in instrument and lessons will not be wasted.

Wind players, on the other hand, are more likely to fall in love with the instrument earlier in their instrumental experience because of the more readily acceptable tone quality in the beginning stages.

These beginnings are significant to the final personality of the performer.

No successful scientific study has ever revealed even the remotest clue as to why anyone takes up the drums.

The Flautist

The performer on the flute considers that his instrument is the most important one in the orchestra. All the proof needed is to point out that the composer's score always has the flute at the top of the page. As if that weren't enough, the flute usually plays higher notes than anybody else with the possible exception of the first violins once in a while. Any flute performer worth his salt believes firmly that the first flute should be concertmaster of the orchestra. At the very least he should have some extra salary and recognition as the leader of not only his own section but all the winds as well.

The flautist is likely an intellectual sort who plays chess, loves lots of women, and always dines well. Women flautists are always beautiful and sexy. When teaching students, flautists insist that the flute be held parallel to the floor, but they never do that themselves. Principal flautists usually weave around a lot whenever they have a solo so that the audience can find them in the orchestra.

The reader may be thinking that I don't know how to spell very well because of my calling the flute player a flautist. This, through tradition (more on this later), is the accepted label given a flute player. The word is Italian from Old Provencal and French usage. I haven't discovered why we don't just say flutist and I will abandon the term from here on.

The Piccoloist

The piccolo player, in literal translation, is playing the "small", as that is what the word means in Italian. The correct term for the instrument is piccolo flute. The performer on this instrument is one of the unfortunate members of the orchestra required to play an instrument not of his or her choosing. This duty is usually imposed on the third flute who is likely the one with the least seniority in the section.

The Oboist

Those who master the oboe feel a huge responsibility to see to the intonation of the complete ensemble and take it as a personal affront if anyone dares to suggest a change of one vibration per second from whatever pitch the oboe happens to be producing at any particular time. I have never heard a reasonable explanation as to why the oboe sounds the pitch for the orchestra tuning, but in a later chapter I present my version of the beginning of that tradition.

Oboists are independent creatures, often gourmet cooks, and have wide interests ranging from music history to obscure Eastern religions. Much of their time away from the orchestra is involved in making reeds for the oboe. Of course they don't really "make" reeds. The reed is a plant that grows in a marsh somewhere. They buy cane that is grown and harvested in some far off exotic land. (Far off exotic cane is always better than local cane even though more expensive and hard to find. I wonder where oboists in those lands get their cane, because I am sure that their tradition demands that good cane must come from far away.) They then carve, scrape, soak in water and tie with colored thread the cane that they have acquired so that it will make the required squawk necessary to produce sound for the oboe.

Making these pieces of cane into useful reeds is a never ending task and can be extremely frustrating. More than once I have seen an oboist at his work bench trying repeatedly to scrape and shape a reed in order to get the correct sound only to give up and destroy what has already consumed considerable time.

A famous oboist is reported to have said, *"Three things I've never completely figured out: women, roulette, and how to get a good reed!"*

The English Hornist

This instrument is an alto oboe, being neither English nor a horn. The player started out on the oboe, got sidetracked to play the English horn when the regular player was ill, and ended up falling in love with this very beautiful, exotic, expressive vamp of an instrument. The English horn performer is a quiet retiring sort who rarely establishes close relationships with other orchestra members. His only interest as far as his colleagues know is his love affair with the instrument.

They would be incredulous if they ever discovered that his recreation away from the orchestra was driving a car at the county fairgrounds in a demolition derby every free week end.

The Clarinetist

The clarinet is the essence of elegance in the orchestral tonal ambiance. Those who master the instrument are elegant people in almost all aspects of their beings. They have the quiet demeanor of one who has made the best possible choice of musical expression and knows within every fiber that his instrument is unsurpassed by any other. The clarinetist is one of the few members of the orchestra who is completely comfortable when invited to social functions put on by the financial supporters of the orchestra. He will go to the exclusive country club soirée and happily rub elbows with those of the upper classes and never even consider the possibility that some in attendance don't know who he is.

The Eb Clarinetist

The Eb Clarinet is the piccolo clarinet and is played by one of the other clarinetists who drew the short straw. Clarinetists, being elegant and refined personalities, practice the part and do what must be done. No fuss is ever heard by other orchestra members about the unfairness, etc.

The Bass Clarinetist

The bass clarinet player never falls in love with the instrument as happens to our previously mentioned English horn player, but being of the elegant sort accepts with equanimity his lateral transfer from the clarinet.

The Bassoonist

This bass of the woodwind family attracts the person who likes a challenge and also likes to be different. The performer develops dexterous thumbs as those are the busy digits because of the arrangement of keys. This player also has to fashion reeds out of cane just as the oboist does. Bassoonists tend to be stubborn and opinionated but usually turn out to be right in the end.

Coleridge in his *The Rime Of The Ancient Mariner* mentions this instrument.

> *"The Wedding-Guest here beat his breast,*
> *For he heard the loud bassoon."*

Fortunately, not all who hear this instrument have the same inclination.

The Contrabassoonist

The contrabassoon is larger and lower pitched than the bassoon. The instrument is rarely used but when needed is played by the only person in town who owns one. This might be the regular second bassoon player, or even someone not a regular member of the orchestra, who has management over a barrel and takes advantage financially of his exclusive position. He resists all attempts by the symphony management or other bassoonists to buy his instrument. Needless to say, he is the one musician in the orchestra with good business sense.

The Brass

A few remarks about brass players in general before proceeding to individual instrumentalists. It must be remembered that brass players produce sound by making an obscene noise produced with the lips into what is essentially a megaphone. One must keep this in mind whenever contemplating the personality of the brass performer. (The word brass is particularly apt in that last sentence.) Players develop the ability to create internal bodily pressures of great strength in order to produce high pitched and loud sounds. When one blows with great force, the resultant effect has two possible outlets, thus the anal sphincter muscle is just as importantly controlled as the muscles contacting the mouthpiece of the instrument.

The Hornist

The French horn is called merely "horn" by all musicians, and the player is the maverick of the orchestra. Consider that the horn is always fingered with the left hand even though most players of the instrument are right handed. Normal people would never put up with such nonsense, but horn players will defend to the death against any ideas of a more practical nature. The horn is king of the mountain in the orchestra. Every horn player knows this. All other sections exist only to enhance the horn or provide necessary contrast. All horn performers humbly acknowledge their superiority to all other musicians. The chairman of the orchestra players' committee will usually be a member of the horn section. If a strike is talked about during contract negotiations, a horn player will be the loudest proponent. If, when the final vote is taken on the new contract, there are three negative votes, two will be from the horn section (the third will be from the last stand of the violas).

Offstage the hornist is likely to show some strong signs of weirdness. It is difficult to generalize in what form this might be manifested but watch for it. Shakespeare may have had an inkling of some special qualities of horn players of his day when he wrote the following in Act IV of *As You Like It.*

> *"Take thou no scorn to wear the horn*
> *It was a crest ere thou wast born,*
> *Thy father's father wore it,*
> *And thy father bore it.*
> *The horn, the horn, the lusty horn*
> *Is not a thing to laugh to scorn."*

It may be going too far to think that all horn players are somehow linked to this kind of activity!

All musicians spend a good deal of their time trying to find a better instrument and thus make the job of music easier. The horn player probably agonizes over this search more than any other instrumentalist. He or she knows that somewhere out there is the perfect horn that is in tune throughout its range and has no notes that are difficult to produce. This instrument also has a tone quality that is far superior to any other ever heard by human ears. Not only that, but it never produces a wrong note or poor attack. It will have the power to dominate the orchestra while playing Wagner and sound delicate as old lace for Haydn. Horns are built in more different arrangements of pipe and valve than any other musical instrument with the possible exception of the pipe organ.

Hornists have had instruments put together in all manner of arrangements in the hope of some improvement. Some players carry more than one instrument to the job in order to match the sound or range to the composition or style required. Despite all this searching for the perfect horn, they are all still played left handed!

The horn player's right hand is placed in the bell of the instrument which somewhat alters the tone quality. This is a tradition begun before the valve was invented, and gives the player the opportunity to vent frustrations with finger signals unseen by the audience.

The Trumpeter

The trumpet player is a person of strong convictions and is a staunch Democrat. The trumpet is mentioned in the Good Book more often than any other instrument and so players consider this a mandate always to make sounds with great conviction. Any composer requiring tentative sounds from this section needs to go back and restudy orchestration. The most avid golfers in the orchestra are probably trumpet players who are almost never caught cheating at counting strokes.

When I was in the music profession, trumpet players almost always used the same Bb instrument for all applications, but today's player has an arsenal of high powered armaments of different bore and stroke for all occasions, including higher pitched trumpets that almost look as if they could fit in the palm of the hand.

Trombonist

The trombone instrumentalist is basically an exhibitionist. Moving the slide to adjust the tubing length and produce the correct notes is always visible to the concert audience and the trombonist would be crushed if asked to use an instrument that had valves like normal brasses do. This person takes great pride in performing on an instrument unlike any other and which is also a source of mystery to his other musician friends. For obscure acoustical reasons, the trombone is the only brass instrument that can always sound exactly in tune in any key. Masters of the instrument never let their colleagues forget this obvious (to them) fact. Subdued muttering often emanates from the trombone section when the oboe sounds the "*A*" for the orchestra to tune.

The Tubaist . . . Tuber . . . The Tuba Player

(I tried to be consistent with titling these sections with the same kind of word to describe the expert who manipulates each instrument. I almost gave up when I came to the trumpet player and this time I admit defeat.) The tuba player is a loner as he almost never has another tuba to keep him company. He is always quiet and unassuming, keeping to himself even off stage. Underneath this quiet exterior seethes a bed of frustration born of real and imaginary persecution because of the scarcity of times when allowed to play. If there is an undetected alcoholic in the orchestra, it is probably the tuba player.

The Tympanist

The tympanist or kettledrummer has a unique position. He takes up more room in the orchestra than three other performers, sits or stands at the center immediately in front of the backdrop or shell and thus knows even better than the conductor who is doing what and when. Nobody ever sees the back of a tympanist and nothing escapes his attention. This gives him insight which is rarely used effectively. Knowing the potential power that is his gives him a sense of importance that can add up to overconfidence. He is more visible to the audience than any other performer except the conductor and this can't help but affect the personality.

A good tympanist is a real asset to an orchestra, but a mediocre one can survive for a long time because conductors are often afraid of them for the above named reasons.

The Percussionist

Percussionists are often apologetic and insecure but hide it very well from everyone. This inferior feeling is based on the knowledge that what they contribute isn't really music, so they are in fact impostors in a musical organization. Added to all of this inner conflict is the fact that when they do their job properly they must usually do it loudly. I suspect that the snare drum roll was inadvertently and unexpectedly invented by an especially nervous drummer who was trying to play written sixteenth notes vivace. Percussionists have to play many different instruments including the so called mallet instruments such as xylophone, orchestra bells, etc. They also may have long periods of inactivity during the concert after which they must resume playing at precisely the correct time.

Most percussionists start learning on the snare drum and a good deal of their early practice time was spent on learning what are called "The Rudiments". These exercises have such wonderful names as thirteen stroke roll, double ratamacue, flam, and paradiddle. When they have mastered all of these they appear before learned judges to demonstrate their skill and then forever after are known as "Rudimental Drummers" having achieved the percussionist's Masters Degree.

Drummers, as they are known in the trade, will buy up old houses and completely renovate them as an investment, sell at a loss and start the process all over again, continuing in this pattern until they get it right. Their other hobby is related to their orchestra work: collecting old pieces of iron with a nice bell-like sound and other oddments of potential percussive paraphernalia.

Second Movement Tacet

They can often be seen walking down the street furtively striking iron street lamp posts, wrought iron gates, and anything else in sight with a drum stick and attending to the sound of the vibratory result. Don't park next to the drummer's car in the parking lot.

The Strings

The string instruments are the backbone of the full symphony orchestra. Without them all that is left is a band, which is a poor substitute for the orchestra. There are many excellent symphonic bands in existence, but several clarinets all playing the same notes can never equal multiple violins on the same part. As mentioned earlier, the string quartet was the basis for the orchestra and adding other violins, violas, and 'cellos to the parts produced a much fuller and lush sound. Strings in large numbers sound well together but woodwinds and brass don't make such nice sounds when put together on the same notes.

The First Violinist

The member of the first violin section is often a disappointed concert violinist. He knows every note the visiting violin soloist will play, is playing, or should have played. He also is sure he could probably play it better than the visiting soloist with a little time to get back in shape and the right breaks. The feeling also is present that playing in an orchestra is really beneath the dignity of someone with his talents and skill. At the very least, he knows he could do a better job than the concertmaster, especially in choosing the proper bowings. (The direction in which the bows move in each string section is never by accident, and much rehearsal time is often taken up with discussions to determine how it will be done in each passage during the concert. Brass, woodwind, and percussion players usually love these long discussions, because they can sit idle while all this is going on.) The first violinist's life soon turns into one of quiet desperation upon recognizing that each year it is harder and takes longer to get ready for the coming season after an all-too-short summer break.

The Second Violinist

This violinist is a quiet, retiring sort of person who is content with his niche in the musical world. *"Just leave me alone"* is the second violinist's motto. Psychiatrists would soon go broke if all the people in the world were second violinists. Their interests are likely to be so varied as to make it impossible to generalize about them. I have known doctors, long-shoremen, postmen, housewives, teachers, machinists, etc., who were also professional second violin players.

The Violist

The complete viola section is made up of people who really wanted to play the violin. Think of all the turmoil that exists in a section where everyone transferred their original musical dream away from their first love, the violin. The melancholic sounds from this section of the orchestra are no accident. Woe to the conductor who wants to get a happy, bright, upbeat, joyful sound from the violas for he has his work cut out for him and he gets no sympathy from me. In the earliest days of symphonic orchestra history, the viola section consisted of those who were too old to be dependable in the violin section anymore.

The Violoncellist

All 'cellists have gypsy blood coursing through their veins. All string players phrase differently than wind instrumentalists because of the bow that makes the strings vibrate. String playing is characterized by crescendi that are totally inappropriate to the logical phrasing. 'Cellists have developed this further than other string players and that is what makes the 'cello section sound like a band of gypsies. Next time that you hear a symphony orchestra, pay particular attention to the 'cellists' rendition of a phrase that has just been presented by other instruments. If you are completely objective and listen carefully you will agree with me. Their gypsy blood will certainly affect the personality in many ways. They like to travel, are inclined to barter when possible, are stubbornly resistant to new ideas and still love music when the rest of the orchestra has had it clear up to here with the conductor and management and aren't even enjoying Mozart anymore.

Notice that the instrument's full name is violoncello. The word "violon" is French for violin and the cello ending means bass in an obscure Italian dialect spoken near Cremona. According to another source, "violone" means a big violin and "cello" is a diminutive so violoncello means "a little big violin". You may take your choice, but the instrument is almost always called "cello".

The Contrabassist

The bass player knows that the most important note in a musical chord is the bottom one, and guess who always plays that note? All bass instrumentalists are conscious of the fact that the bass preceded the violoncello in Haydn's orchestra and thus harbor some inner resentment at the 'cellos seeming superior attitude. They are all convinced that the bass section could play all the 'cello parts and that they would sound much better also. In fact the bass is the one surviving member of the viol family of instruments which preceded the violin family. This knowledge of instrumental music history gives the bass performer a reasonable excuse to feel superior to all other symphony musicians.

There is one fact about playing this instrument that practitioners try to keep to themselves: It takes special skill and practice in listening in order to hear pitches in the low frequency that they sound, and most other musicians, especially conductors, can't really tell whether or not they are playing in tune.

There actually was a first chair bass player in one of the highest ranking orchestras who seriously insisted each year at contract time that he be named concertmaster. I never met a contrabass instrumentalist who saw any reason to regard that as remarkable.

As you watch the contrabass section, look for the way they hold their bows. There are two kinds: the German bow and the French bow. The French bow looks like a fatter 'cello bow and the German bow is very close to the original viol bow. Most orchestras will have players of both persuasions in the section. The instrument is traditionally played while standing, but nowadays many players have grown lazy and like to sit on a high stool even during concerts.

The Harpist

Like the tuba player, the harpist is usually alone in the orchestra although there are some compositions that require two players. This performer is always the first to arrive at either rehearsal or concert because it takes a long time to tune the instrument. Unlike the piano which uses steel wire strings, the harp uses soft strings originally of animal intestinal origin but now of synthetic materials. These will get out of tune from merely transporting the instrument or even placing it in a location in the theater or rehearsal hall where there is a draft. Harpists become fanatics about their instruments because of the difficulty involved in transportation and care. Some have been known to carry a portable electric heater in order to overcome a less than desirable drafty placement in the orchestra pit.

We all have marveled at the harpist dexterously plucking away, but we usually miss the most difficult manipulations because they are carried out by the feet. There are seven pedals to be manipulated to change the strings, and each string can be changed to sound one of three different notes. The strings are color coded so the harpist can find the right place to pluck. Once a harpist I knew was placed on stage during a performance where there were different lighting effects taking place. This effectively made it impossible to identify the proper strings and caused the performer great anguish to say the least.

I am not sure that harpists have a life away from the harp, although I did know one who was a yachtsman of great skill in navigation and other nautical matters.

As mentioned earlier, generalities such as these are bound to be wrong most of the time, but I find the variety of personalities that make up the symphonic ensemble to be fascinating. When the orchestra is at its best, the music is a single entity born of the talents and hard work of up to one hundred individuals. All these people have only two things in common: interpreting the piece of music they are producing at the moment and universal discontent with the conductor.

An analysis of the function of the musicians in an orchestra will show that there are at least three different expectations depending on the instrument played and the position in the section. Members of the string sections, with the exception of the principal in each section, are best characterized as drones in a bee-hive. They have a specific job to do which, if done correctly, insures that no attention is called to them as individuals. Some very fine string players are poor orchestra material because of an inability to blend into the woodwork of the section.

All wind players are required to play parts for which they alone are responsible. This means that they must be note perfect as well as blending with all others in their section. All good string players know when to back off a bit and let the super-honchos in their section furnish the clarity to a difficult passage. This does not mean that they did not practice diligently and thoroughly, but that they have the good sense to recognize where their own abilities are strongest.

The third type of instrumentalist is the percussion player whose work might seem the easiest and least important to the casual listener and observer. The percussionist is the one member of the orchestra who is expected to be proficient on many different instruments and always with impeccable rhythm, even when the conductor has varied the beat three times in as many measures.

All of these men and women are dedicated to being the best musicians possible, through the manipulation of their chosen instruments, and have the added burden of having to do it simultaneously with about one hundred others. All of this superb musicianship and coordination must be executed precisely with the conductor, with whom they may disagree musically.

The end result of all these different personalities interacting during several rehearsals, and finally the formal concert, is a unified performance of some music composed by someone known to them usually only through reputation and not directly. As I mentioned, there is likely to be disagreement between players and conductor as well as between individual players about many aspects of reproducing the music. A good conductor can persuade the musicians to a unified result that ensures a faithful presentation of the composer's intentions.

If all problems are handled by the conductor with respect for the musicians' musical integrity, the music making can be great fun.

Chapter III

It's Really Much Better Than It Sounds

When a contemporary piece of music was programmed for the orchestra in which I was playing, I was always reminded of what Mark Twain said about contemporary music: *"It's really much better than it sounds!"* Of course, he was talking about Wagner, but this suggested the title of this chapter on acoustics and some related matters.

Sound is audible vibration. Regular organized vibrations produce music, irregular disorganized vibrations produce noise. Very few musical tones consist of only one frequency of vibrations, but have several tones occurring at the same time. These other sounds are weak compared to the one that we recognize as a particular pitch, and are called "overtones". Some instruments produce many overtones, and others produce fewer, or an uneven selection of overtones. Our ears detect these differences and thus help us to identify the particular instrument producing the sound.

There are diagrams, graphs, and other visual aids in all music encyclopedias that attempt to explain about overtones, but there is a much simpler experiment that you can perform that will demonstrate the phenomenon. In order to understand, however, you need to keep in mind another characteristic of sound waves. This is the fact that sound waves cause objects that they contact to vibrate in sympathy with them. Your ear-drums resonating to vibrations in the air is a good example.

This sympathetic vibration can be used to demonstrate the overtones in your own voice. Simply walk over to your piano, lift the lid: the topmost lid on an upright, or the large slanting cover on a grand piano. Hold the loud pedal down to lift the dampers from the strings, and shout "*Hey!*" into the piano. The piano strings that match the overtones of your voice will vibrate in sympathy and reproduce the tone quality of your voice. Have other members of the family try it and notice the difference in tone. If you don't have a piano, go to your neighborhood church and try it there, preferably when there is no service in progress. Don't try to use the organ at the church, however, because organs are very unsympathetic and obstinate and won't cooperate.

For those who wish to learn more about the overtones of instruments, I recommend the book *Horns, Strings & Harmony* by Arthur Benade.

Starting with the flute, there is no reason why the flute should make any sound at all! It has no reed, the players' lips do not buzz, nothing makes the sound. I have been told that it is the same principle as blowing across the mouth of a bottle to produce an eerie hoot. So I guess the flute is an eerie hooter at best. The clarinet has a single reed that vibrates to close and open the entrance to the instrument itself. The oboe and bassoon have double reeds which open and close against each other to create the vibrating air column.

So much for the noisemaker parts of the woodwinds. They all differentiate the required pitches more or less in similar fashion, that is, by closing and opening holes in the pipe attached to the basic noisemaker. The closer to the noisemaker that the vibrations run into a hole in the pipe where the air can leak out, the greater their astonishment and consequently the higher they scream. I have heard other ridiculous explanations of the phenomenon but this is more accurate, believe me.

The basic sound of the brasses is produced by an obscene noise made with the lips into a very unsanitary funnel-shaped mouthpiece. The resulting moist vibrations pass on into a long pipe with a flaring other end called a bell. The length of that pipe determines the pitches that emanate. Notice that I referred to pitches in the plural because the performer can invoke the god of physics that lives inside the pipe by pushing harder on the mouthpiece or cup thus impacting the lips to produce a note further up the overtone series. Some performers try to spread the heresy that the facial muscles must be trained to adjust the tension on the lips to pick off the various notes available in the aforementioned series. (Too ridiculous to justify with comment!) Just watch some brass players and judge for yourself. The muscles that must be developed are all in the left biceps.

When the brass first forced their way into the orchestra, the valve (to be described later) hadn't been invented yet. Thus composers stuck to the overtone series in their compositions when writing brass parts. (Any bugle call will demonstrate the overtone series.) Some simply marvelous music was written and performed using this system, but there is always a smart-aleck who makes life impossible for the other members of his profession. Anton Joseph Hampel (died 1771), a Dresden horn player, discovered that by using his hand in the bell he could more or less produce all the diatonic notes of the scale. Naturally word got around to the composers who immediately began staying up nights to write music for horns that used the complete scale and completely ruined a good thing for all horn players right down to the present. Supposedly, before Hampel's hand-in-the-bell system, the horns in the orchestra were played with the bell straight up in the air.

The string instruments produce sound by causing a string under tension to vibrate either by plucking, hitting or scraping. The scraping part of the instrument is called the bow as in bow and arrow. This bow has many horse hairs stretched between its two ends. Horse hair has a rough surface so that when scraped across the tensioned string, the string is alternately grabbed and released causing it to vibrate. Brave orchestra players use rosin on the bow to increase the friction. Timid players might wish to use soap for the opposite effect.

All the string instruments in the orchestra family have four strings with the exception of the contrabass which may have another lower string to increase the range downward. To produce diatonic notes between the basic pitches of each string, the player presses the string down forcibly against a hardwood board thus shortening its length and producing a sound with higher pitch. The basic pitch of a vibrating string depends on tension, length, thickness, and the material of which it is made.

The instruments of the orchestra were developed to their present level of relative perfection over many years. Some of the history of this development is fascinating, some is not.

According to mythology, the flute was invented by Minerva. She was the Roman goddess of wisdom, although she did some foolish things besides inventing the flute. She was patroness of the arts and trades. She had no mother, but sprang fully armed from the head of Jupiter. She played the flute for the pleasure of all the other gods, but made strange faces while playing which caused Cupid to laugh. This enraged Minerva so much that she threw the instrument away and it fell down to earth to be found and retrieved by the satyr Marsyas, who became thus the first earthly flute player. He blew upon it and became so enamored of the sound and his ability to produce and control it that he challenged the god Apollo to a musical contest or audition.

Apollo was the god of archery, prophecy, music, and healing. As the leader of the muses, he was given the lyre (predecessor of the harp) which Mercury invented and, in turn, gave music to woman when she was invented. He was the father of Orpheus, another musician. (But I digress.)

At the ensuing audition for first chair in the universe, Marsyas lost out to the reigning god and Apollo punished him by flaying him alive. Needless to say, the musicians' union was not active at that time or his punishment would have been contested. I wonder if this early flute player being a satyr has had any influence on the morals of later performers on the flute.

The original flute was a simple tube with enough holes that could be covered by one performer's fingers and still produce a chromatic scale by lifting single or combinations of fingers. The holes had to be placed where fingers could reach them, but that wasn't where the god of acoustics decreed that they should be for good intonation. Various flute players experimented with levers that would allow the holes to be placed according to acoustic needs rather than that of convenience to the fingers.

Theobald Boehm (1793-1881) finally tired of struggling with the imperfect eight keyed flute that had been developed and which he played in the Royal Orchestra at Munich. In 1832 he developed a system using ring keys to cover fourteen holes. He later also made other improvements, many of which were adapted to other woodwind instruments, especially the clarinet.

The horn and trumpet players, when they played only the overtones (bugle call notes), had to have an instrument built to play in the key that the orchestra was playing at the moment. During one single concert the orchestra might play in many different keys, in fact the key might change during the course of one piece of music. The brass player would then have to have with him an instrument for each key that would be used. When the change of key happened within one piece, it might be difficult to discard one instrument and pick up another in time, especially as horns don't respond well until warmed up with the breath.

In order to cut down on the number of instruments that a brass player had to carry to a gig (musical engagement either rehearsal, concert, or later recording session), brass instrument makers began to make trumpets and horns with a removable section of tubing that could be replaced with a coiled tube of different length than that removed. This made the instrument play in a different key.

Some obscure instrument maker had the brilliant idea of adapting the water faucet to make a tap that could redirect air into different tubes. At first he only wanted to make it possible for the player to change from one key to a related key and then back again, so only one tap was needed. This tap could be located wherever was convenient for the instrument maker to place it, because there would be enough time for the player to remove the instrument from the lips, turn the little handle and proceed in the new key.

Once this innovation became common knowledge, other instrument makers began to experiment with the idea, using different kinds of taps or valves as they came to be known, and adding more than just one to the instrument. There were at least three different styles of valve that were tried and today there are still two types that are common, the rotary and the piston valve.

It was found that the gaps between all the usable bugle notes could be filled in with just three valves, and these were arranged to be worked by the fingers of the right hand on the trumpet and by the left hand on the horn. Why did horn players use the left hand for the valves? Because they had all adopted Hampel's technique of using the right hand in the bell to produce the diatonic notes, and they saw no reason to abandon this technique perfected by many hours of practice to use a technological innovation that could fail at some critical spot in the performance.

The concert attendee probably never thinks about the basis for the pitch in the orchestra unless there are glaring discrepancies between performers. The fact is that orchestras play to a higher standard of pitch today than they did two hundred years ago. (A musician friend of mine insists that in using the terms high and low to describe different notes, we are using the wrong descriptive words. We should instead use fast and slow, because the speed of the vibrations determines pitch. Thus a high note is produced by faster vibrations than a low note.)

It is thought that in the 1700's the pitch for "A" was as low as 422 vibrations per second. As early as the year 1834 attempts were made to establish the standard of pitch by declaring that "A" would have a value of 440 vibrations per second, which is standard now, but in 1859 the French adopted 435 as their standard, later copied by other European countries within a few years. The English did not agree and went clear up to 450 vibrations for their standard. The importance of these discrepancies may escape the non-musician.

Think of the problems for a traveling soloist playing with orchestras in France then going across the channel to England. It would almost feel like playing in a different key. You may well ask, "Can't they just tune to the resident orchestra?" This sounds like an easy solution, but musicians get so used to the pitches used all the time that it would be difficult and would cause confusion to the ear.

An even more important factor to the player of woodwind instruments is that the spacing of the holes bored in the instrument is dependent on knowing what the basic pitch will be when the instrument is played. Some conductors have insisted that their orchestras tune to a higher pitch than standard to achieve a more "bright" sound without a thought to the difficulties imposed on the players whose instruments are built to a different standard. Sometimes I think that the conductor who does this is only trying to recapture the way music used to sound to him before he lost the ability to hear the higher overtones. All of us gradually lose the upper sounds in the aging process, and this may even cause some very fine musicians to play slightly above pitch as they age.

Not all instruments of the orchestra are pitched in the same key. Or in other words, each instrument playing a scale with no sharps or flats does not play the same scale as every other one.

The violin has strings tuned to, in ascending order, G, D, A, and E. Starting a scale on any of these open strings (no fingers shortening the length) produces scales in sharp keys named after the string started on. Obviously the violin can play in any key, but these sharp keys are generally easier. The other bowed strings are similar but we don't usually say that the string instruments are basically in a particular key.

The flute is in the key of C although there have been some manufactured in other keys. The alto flute is pitched in G, and the bass flute is pitched in C, an octave below the standard instrument. I have seen an Eb flute, but I never saw one used in the orchestra.

The oboe is also in C but the English horn (alto oboe) is in the key of F. The music for the English horn is transposed so that the oboe player can push the same keys to play each instrument. A written C is fingered the same way on each instrument, but on the English horn sounds an F.

The clarinet is normally pitched in Bb, but all symphony clarinetists must also have an instrument pitched in A because some composers write the parts in that transposition if their composition is in a sharp key.

The bassoon is really an F instrument, but its parts are not transposed, because most of the time it plays in the bass clef and all instruments that play in bass clef, with one exception, read the actual notes sounding. For high notes the bassoon uses other clefs, but there is still no transposing.

Up until the 1940's, symphony trumpet players used a Bb instrument even though the parts might have been written for trumpets in a different key. The player then had to transpose the part mentally as he played. In more recent years trumpet players have acquired, and learned to be comfortable playing a whole golf bag of different keyed trumpets, and may even change to a different one within the same composition.

The horn parts in modern compositions are always written in the key of F, because the F horn became standard in the orchestra probably about the beginning of this century. (Mozart preferred the sound of the horn pitched in Eb which, because of the lower standard pitch in use then, sounded as a D horn would today, thus the tone quality would be different than we are accustomed to hearing now.)

Early composers wrote the horn parts in C (no sharps or flats) and told the player what key his instrument must be in.

Trombones are pitched in Bb but play in bass clef most of the time, and so read in C. All instruments that read in the bass clef have their parts written as if they are pitched in C. The only instrument in the orchestra that reads bass clef, but does not sound the actual notes written is the contrabass which sounds an octave (eight notes) lower. (I once went to dinner with a contrabassist known for his tremendous appetite, who proceeded to order an octave of spare ribs. This probably has nothing to do with acoustics.)

I actually heard the following announcement made just before a concert by a non-musician introducing the conductor.

> *"I hope that you will enjoy the program, but I have been*
> *told that the agnostics in this room are very bad!"*

Well, at least some of this chapter was about acoustics.

Chapter IV

Do You Really Get Paid For Doing That?

or

Don't Quit Your Day Job Just Yet

This chapter is a sonata of several movements, but on the theme of the working musician trained in the classical style. The first title of this chapter was a question seriously asked of me once by a college-educated professional in a different field. The secondary title is the punch line to the story of a young musician upon finishing his first gig who asks an older colleague, "*How did I do?*"

I am always surprised when I discover that many professional symphony performers don't know who Theodore Thomas was or the important role that he played in the spread of symphony orchestra literature throughout the United States.

Thomas was born in Germany in 1835. His father was a violinist and taught him violin also. He first played in public at the age of six and was brought to America at ten. He was soon doing orchestra work in New

York on the violin as well as playing second horn in the Navy Band. (His father was first horn.)

One of the orchestral engagements that he frequently had was as a first violinist with Julien's orchestra. (See Chapter V.) He found the experience to be a perplexing affront to his musical sensibilities and determined to work toward having his own orchestra that would bring good, tastefully performed music to his adopted country.

In 1862 he achieved this goal with the formation of his own orchestra which toured extensively wherever the railroads could transport them. Each year the tour was expanded as the rail system was extended, eventually reaching even to the Pacific Coast. His orchestra numbered only 54 men, but played a large repertoire of Mozart, Haydn and other recognized composers. He introduced Richard Strauss' music to America even before it was well known in Germany. His orchestra played many works by Tchaikovsky, Dvorak, Bruckner, and Saint-Saens that had never been heard in America before.

He taught people so well to appreciate good music that those in communities with enough resources didn't want to wait for his once-a-year tour and began forming their own local orchestras that could produce concerts several times a year. The eventual result of this development was that each year there were fewer cities where his orchestra could enjoy a full house to pay the traveling expenses and payroll. Reportedly he paid his musicians well and had access to the best musicians of the time.

The Theodore Thomas Orchestra's yearly itinerary became known as the "Thomas Highway". One of its frequent stops was in Philadelphia where he was invited in 1876 to preside over the musical festivities of their Centennial Exposition to celebrate the signing of the Declaration of Independence. An admirer and advocate of Richard Wagner's music, he commissioned Wagner to compose a special *"Grand Centennial March"* for $5000 to be paid for by the Women's Centennial Committee. The score Wagner sent was reportedly unplayable trash and had to be rewritten by Thomas before it could be performed. (The Philadelphia orchestra wasn't formally organized until 1900.)

Finally the time arrived when there were not enough cities left without their own orchestras to make the Thomas Orchestra's tour financially successful. About the time that Thomas realized this, some Chicago business people thought that the time had come to have their own orchestra so they approached him with an offer to bring his orchestra there and make Chicago their home. This offer included Thomas being engaged as the resident musical director and most of his musicians having agreed to locate there also. Thus did the Chicago Symphony begin in 1891.

Thomas' desire to educate the American people musically resulted in the formation of orchestras in all cities where he had been heard in the American nation. For this reason, all professional symphony musicians should know of him and his efforts that indirectly furnished the opportunity for their own employment.

What I have written so far is about the symphony orchestra, but there are other ways that a "classically" trained musician earns a living. The ballet and opera orchestras are symphony orchestras scaled down in the string sections so that they can fit in the orchestra pit, that big hole in front of the stage. There are cities where the scheduled events are arranged so that the same musicians can work symphony, opera and ballet, and sometimes musicians might be under contract for all three under one management. There are also areas where all three are so busy that separate orchestras are needed.

Working in the pit is different than being the center of attention on stage, but the music is much the same. The conductor now earns his salt on these jobs, as coordination between stage and pit is essential.

Good ballet conductors can bring a rhythmic steadiness to the music that is often ignored in other kinds of performances. The result is graceful, tasteful music seldom heard in any other setting. One often hears ballet music performed on stage or on recordings when it is apparent to anyone with experience in the pit that the conductor has never conducted a ballet performance because the elegance is not present in the rhythm.

Opera orchestra work can be very tiring. Sometimes the torture goes on for as much as four hours with only short breaks. People in offices or even factory workers don't see anything hard about those four hours in comparison to their own work hours, but believe me it is no picnic. I have done both.

If you are an office worker, pretend that you must hold the computer keyboard with one hand, unsupported by a desk, at arms length while you type sixty words per minute with the other hand. There will be periods of time from five to twenty minutes where you cannot put it down for even five seconds. This is comparable to what the violinist or viola player must do.

Another kind of musical employment is often available to the local musician. Every year there are traveling companies that bring music theater to the provinces. These shows usually originate in New York and include only certain key players for the orchestra, the rest being hired locally. Usually there is only one rehearsal before the first performance. The instrumentalists carried with the traveling company will vary depending on the demands of the particular musical but might include the concertmaster, first trumpet, and a pianist, for example.

Once or twice a year an ice skating spectacular may arrive in town to furnish a week or two of work. This will not furnish work for many symphony personnel, because the music is written for stage band with full saxophone and brass sections plus a few strings. The music is quite demanding and also requires that the player know how to play the rhythm as stage bands do which is quite different from playing Mozart. There will be only one rehearsal, usually only covering the hardest parts of the performance so that the musician is sight reading a lot in the first performance.

Another bit of fun occurs when one is engaged to play for a well known singer making the national circuit. Here again the musician may have to phrase the rhythm differently than in symphony or classic style. Again, some essential instrumentalists will travel with the artist and there will be only one rehearsal.

When I first began in the music profession, I found myself sitting in an orchestra containing musicians with a wide range of training and experience, and from whom I learned a great deal. Some had been trained in Europe in the best conservatories and by well known teachers there. Many had been members of pit orchestras that played daily for silent movies. There were those who had played with the staff orchestras with early radio stations. In fact the leaders of some of those pit and radio orchestras were playing in the orchestra that I joined. To hear these men talk of their experiences was rewarding and valuable to a new player.

I have previously referred in an offhand way to the musician's union. As I write this (1994), the unions seem to be in decline in America in almost every field. Young people that I talk with in all kinds of work seem to be almost universally anti-union. There is little knowledge of the working conditions that prevailed before unions were organized. There have been so many times when the media, in covering union management negotiations or disputes, seem to favor the management side. The reason this might be true seems obvious: unions don't normally advertise. Businesses advertise, and the media exists in order to make money through selling advertising.

I don't mean to imply that unions are always right and management is always wrong in any encounter. Union policy can be, and sometimes is, very ill-advised and unfair. On the other hand, professional musicians would not exist if the musician's union had not been in existence as the orchestras were formed and developed in this century. Without the union we would have been playing for free beers!

The histories of many of the orchestras in this country contain incidents of unrest and even strikes. My own experiences in music and other work over many years has reinforced an opinion about such affairs. I feel strongly that whenever a labor dispute occurs, the true beginning of the problem is rarely, if ever, mentioned in the media. The main emphasis in disputes, according to the media, seems to be over money matters, but the workers (musicians in this case) often demand compensation when they are really unhappy over other matters and can see no other relief for their frustrations.

Even the major orchestras in the first half of the 20th century did not offer full employment year 'round to their musicians, so the players had to depend on other music jobs or private teaching in order to live during part of the year. Salaries during the playing season were low in comparison to other professions requiring the same amount of study to reach proficiency.

The following story may give some insight to the way musicians have had to struggle for their desire to have some control of their lives. This story is true as well as I can remember the events, which occurred many years ago. I apologize to any who may know this story and remember it differently. To any of you I can only say, "*You may be right!*"

Many years ago in a fair city much like many others we all know, existed a symphony orchestra with a long history of superior musical accomplishment. Even during the depression years, the orchestra maintained a healthy existence both musically and financially. After World War II the resident conductor moved on to greener pastures and a replacement was hired by the largest financial supporter of the sustaining fund. As might be suspected, this financial expert knew little about music and perhaps even less about proper conductor qualifications.

The conductor's shortcomings were so glaring to the orchestra personnel that even the normally most docile of the members were easily persuaded, near the end of the second season, to sign a petition for his removal which was finally presented to the symphony board of directors. The board's response was that it was really too late to secure a proper replacement for next season so there would be no season. The conductor could read the writing on the wall better than he could a musical score so he resigned and left town.

There was a conductor of some talent and good European training who was presenting concerts in a neighboring community. He was known to many of the symphony players because he frequently hired them when necessary to fill in key places in his own orchestra. This conductor had financial support for his own concerts and set out to transfer that support to the symphony with himself as the musical director. This plan was put into effect and the season was on again.

This financial support was not enough to sustain the needs of the budget, and the adverse publicity of the players' petition and subsequent management decision to cancel the season resulted in very poor ticket sales revenue. The newspapers had covered all these events with typical support for management. The musicians were faced with unemployment and since the symphony management had never paid into the state unemployment system, even though they were supposed to, there was no financial help available that other workers normally call upon. The musicians met and agreed to petition their union to allow them to play for gate receipts, to form their own corporation to handle internal affairs, and to distribute wages according to their own schedule. The union agreed to this and the season was completed.

After a rather bleak season financially, the symphony society reorganized and tried to hire the musicians for the next year. The musicians had had a taste of controlling some aspects of their musical lives and offered to sell their services as an organized entity. The management tried to hire other local musicians to start the season but were unable to form an ensemble that would be acceptable to any desirable prospective conductor.

Negotiations between this new musicians' co-op, the union and the management were finally completed and the season launched. A conductor of worldwide reputation was engaged and completed two successful seasons. During this time the officers of the co-op declared positions open, held auditions and otherwise worked amicably with the conductor on personnel and other problems. The co-op was paid a fee per service which was divided up among the members according to their own payment schedule.

Shortly before the third season was to start, unavoidable circumstances made it impossible for the conductor to return. (Some musicians felt that those circumstances had been arranged. Subsequent events seemed to lend credence to the idea.) Management delayed the opening of the season in order to arrange a complete season with guest conductors. This was done and the season completed.

The next season was to be handled the same way, but one conductor was engaged for more than one concert and was clearly under consideration for a permanent position. The players co-op board interviewed this man to find out his feelings about the peculiar local arrangement. He indicated that he saw no reason why the co-op should not continue and even expressed enthusiasm at the concept, having been familiar with a similar effort in a foreign country. When the management approached the players co-op board seeking endorsement of the prospective permanent conductor, a positive vote was recommended to the membership and passed.

The next season was a getting acquainted time and ended amicably. The following season proceeded to a close and the conductor asked for an orchestra meeting. At this meeting the conductor expressed in very strong terms that the arrangement was not working and that if the co-op was not disbanded immediately, he would leave town and furthermore he would see to it that none of the orchestra members would ever play professionally again anywhere! He then left the room and discussion began.

Many of the members were all for going back to the traditional role of playing music and let management and conductor handle all other matters. This was all they had known most of their lives, and any other involvement on their part was stressful which made it more difficult to do the job of making good music. Others were convinced that the conductor could, in fact, carry out the blacklisting threats. Music was their whole life and they had no doubt that disbanding was the only choice. Idealists in the crowd tried to point out that the co-op did still have a strong position if the members would agree to stand firm. A motion to disband was passed.

Through the years previous to this crisis the orchestra had been a cohesive entity that put on Christmas parties for members and their children, enjoyed other social functions together, etc. As a result of this emotional meeting and the vote to disband, many friendships were destroyed, members would not speak to others, and some even developed serious emotional problems. One first chair player's emotional illness resulted in his leaving the orchestra, never to play again. Another player committed suicide some months later.

The traditional way of controlling the musical and financial life of the instrumentalist lives on.

Chapter V

Conductors, Critics and Other Trivia

If the reader has reached this point without skipping anything, the impression has no doubt formed that I have a low regard for conductors. I do not mean to imply that all conductors are incompetent, for that is obviously not true. What I object to is our cultural habit of wishing to elevate certain jobs in society to a level beyond deserving. Without competent leadership, no orchestra would rise to prominence. Competent leadership implies good basic musical ability and training which every successful symphony musician must have, but not all instrumentalists have the desire to learn the few extra skills necessary to conduct. Before exploring those skills let's look at the history of conducting and conductors.

In the earliest operas the director of the musical proceedings sat in the center of the orchestra pit at the harpsichord. He played all the accompaniments on the harpsichord for the recitatives (the solo parts in early opera) and could be seen by singers on stage and all musicians in the pit. From this position he conducted when necessary. When the orchestra moved on stage, the stroke oar of the violins (concertmaster) would start the orchestra on each piece and they stayed together by *LISTENING* to each other. In all fairness, the orchestra was small. This must not always have been satisfactory because conductors soon began to appear on stage.

Lully (1632-1687) is often credited with being the first to conduct with the baton. He was born in Italy of poor parents, was taught violin by a Franciscan monk, and brought to France by a nobleman to entertain the noble person's equally noble lady friend. Lully set to music a satirical poem about the noble lady and got himself fired from the court band.

He later directed the king's own orchestra for Louis XIV and also first brought horns into the orchestra. His baton was rather large by today's standards and he managed, in a fit of anger at some musical aberration, to strike himself in the foot and cause a fatal wound. (Served him right for bringing in the horns.) He was a talented and prolific composer, and is credited with inventing French opera which is less fancy than Italian opera.

Julien prepares to conduct Beethoven

Most early conductors were composers and stood in front of the orchestra at rehearsal to make corrections and show what their intentions were in the composition. I suspect that their conducting at the concert was primarily to let the audience see who was responsible for all the commotion. The conductor-composer had justification for being up front and receiving acclaim for what had just been presented. When a musician steps out from the orchestra to be of help in preparing and presenting the orchestra in concert, he is only one step above the concertmaster who is the first violin section leader.

Among the pioneer conductors were the composers Ludwig Spohr, Carl Maria von Weber, and Felix Mendelssohn. It is reported that prior to Spohr the only baton was a rolled up sheet of music. To Mendelssohn belongs the honor of setting up the format of the symphony concert that still prevails today. We also owe him a debt of gratitude for his revival of Bach's music which was little known outside of a small area up to that time.

Conducting has now become a specialized art and the conductor has been raised to a level in the minds of the audience beyond deserving. I have played for many conductors who deserved recognition and some who did not.

Louis Julien (1812-1860) is the father of a school of conducting that is all too prevalent today. He formed an orchestra in new York in mid-nineteenth century to put on concerts featuring circus-type stunts and combining peasant dance music with Beethoven. He conducted from a raised throne at center stage facing the audience. Before conducting classical compositions, an attendant would bring out white gloves on a satin pillow. These were put on with the appropriate pomp and ceremony. His concerts usually ended with a piece of his own composition called *"The Fireman's Quadrille"*. During this piece, the theater was purposely set on fire. The fire company was of course waiting in the wings and, with great élan, performed the necessary extinguishing procedures as the orchestra performed. Fainting women were said to be a common adjunct. Julien's final years were spent in a mental hospital in Paris. (Honestly, I did not make this up!)

Now I am sure that you will say that such things could never occur today, and how can I say that he is the ancestor of some of today's conductors? Just remember that the conductor's job is only to unify and guide the musicians, not to impress the audience. Analyze what you see them doing during the concert. Are they only directing in ways which are helpful to the members of the orchestra?

And now to the conductor's job description.

> The conductor is above all else a musician and:
> *must* have score reading skill.
> *must* have knowledge of all the
> instruments of the orchestra.
> *must* be able to transmit
> his musical ideas with baton
> and by explanation.
> *must* know how to organize and manage
> an effective and efficient rehearsal.
> *must* have musical ideas consistent with
> traditional performances.
> *must* be familiar with all composers
> common to the standard
> orchestral programming.
> *must* be comfortable with the social
> obligations necessary to insure
> financial support.
> *must* have and exhibit good musical
> taste.
> *should* be a teacher (*note change from
> must to should*).
> *should* be sensitive to the musicality
> and feelings of the musicians in
> the orchestra.

Most audiences, and some conductors, don't realize that the conductor's primary work has all been done at rehearsal before the concert.

The wild gyrations, soulful looks, elaborate cues and the generation of profuse perspiration at the concert are all unnecessary and thus are only to impress the audience. In other words, this is merely a somewhat subdued Julien-type of behavior. Some conductors have a stage hand come and remove their music stand for a performance of some piece that they have memorized which is just a variation on Julien's white gloves bit. The reason he knows the piece that well may possibly be explained by the fact that he had to listen to a recording over and over in order to learn how it goes. I knew a pianist with great score reading ability who was hired by a famous conductor to play new scores for him so that he could figure out how to conduct them.

Audiences are generally willing to give the conductor much credit which he may not deserve. There have been conductors who took an orchestra that was not particularly well-known and, through good teaching, transformed it into a fine musical ensemble. There also have been conductors who took over fine musical ensembles and immediately began to replace the first chair members with supposedly better musicians from their last orchestra. A competent conductor does not need to do this and is only demonstrating a lack of confidence in his teaching ability.

There may be another reason why a new resident conductor might replace most or all of the first chair players. He may feel this is the quickest way to gain the loyal support of the orchestra members, by placing in charge of each section those people who owe their new jobs to him.

There is a story told of a first chair flute player of well deserved renown who found himself trapped by a dowager at a tea for symphony supporters.

Dowager, "*Oh, I just love to hear you play! Tell me, what profession would you have chosen if you had not been a musician?*"

"*Oh, that's easy,*" was his reply. "*I would have been a conductor!*"

Another story is told of a similarly well-known horn player referring to the treacherous nature of his instrument. "*I spent years of my life, and thousands of dollars on lessons and instruments, but next time I would just buy a little stick for fifteen cents that never makes any mistakes!*"

Newspaper critics are a never ending source of wonder to the symphony orchestra performer. Their usual pattern of criticism seems to be that if they liked the performance, the conductor did a superb piece of interpretation. If they didn't like the performance, the musicians were not able to come up to the fine directional leadership of the conductor. I remember concerts where we, the players, managed to salvage performances that were poorly rehearsed and ineptly conducted. We never had any thanks from critics, conductors or anybody else.

There must be some reason for music critics to exist, but the need for them is a mystery to me. We musicians were often amused by what they wrote, and perhaps furnishing amusement is sufficient reason for their existence. It is frightening to think that many concert attendees might take their comments seriously. Critics' assessments of musical events are more often wrong than chance can account for. Sometimes we would read criticism of other musical events in town and wonder if we had missed a marvelous performance because a critic had panned the concert badly. If the same critic praised a musical performance, we were thankful that we had not chosen to attend it.

Someone observed that a critic is little more than a dog looking for a hydrant! Brendan Behan said, "*Critics are like eunuchs in a harem. They know how it's done, they've seen it done every day, but they're unable to do it themselves.*"

Sir Thomas Beecham once labeled critics, "*Drooling, driveling, doleful, depressing, drips*".

Igor Stravinsky wrote, "*I had another dream the other day about music critics. They were small and rodent-like with padlocked ears, as if they had stepped out of a painting by Goya.*

Stravinski's dream of a music critic

I have also heard it said that a critic is one who never actually goes to battle yet afterward comes out shooting the wounded.

The orchestra manager is often a source of frustration to the musician. This person has the financial obligations of the orchestra as top priority and may or may not have any knowledge or interest in music or musicians. My recollections of dealings with orchestra managers are nearly all negative. I was exploited by business managers at least twice during my professional orchestral playing years. Both instances were cases concerning verbal agreements arrived at for services beyond contracted services that were not honored afterward. There is no way to take back music already performed. Very few people have the time and energy to master a musical instrument and also study how the economic world operates and learn how to manipulate it to advantage. I remember a few who did but most of them left the music field after a few years.

Most professional musicians learned the mechanics necessary to manipulate their particular instrument by studying with a teacher on a one-to-one basis. The same, or maybe a different, teacher taught the instrumentalist what he needed to know about music. Some teachers are good instrumental players themselves and some are not. Some of them are good players, but poor teachers, and some are mediocre players, but good teachers. I have known some very fine instrumental performers who studied with inadequate teachers but managed to rise above bad input and succeed on their own.

There is a virus that seems to infect many teachers whether they are good or poor. This disease manifests itself in making the teacher feel that a successful student never need study with anyone else and should remain dependent on the one teacher for all musical development the rest of the student's life, even after he has become a first chair player in a famous orchestra or a concert solo artist. A teacher may even become a hanger-on at all performances as if the student (even though now fifty years old) still needs advice before each performance.

Thus far I have not made a distinction between amateur and professional orchestras. I was amazed some years ago to find that there were supposedly well-educated people who did not realize that musicians in the symphony orchestra were paid a salary for their services. Of course there are also many amateur orchestras, sometimes even in the same area, where a full-time professional group exists. There are also professional part-time and semi-professional groups where only some members are paid. My own first pay-for-play experience was with an orchestra that only had a four or five concert season.

After leaving the professional music scene, I tried playing with a few different amateur orchestras because I really do enjoy experiencing the orchestral literature first hand, so to speak. I found that I didn't enjoy playing with some of them because of the conductors. I had absolutely no problem with the instrumental musicians, even when skills were minimal, and often there were amateurs in the group who were every bit as good as the best professionals.

The story is told of a wealthy man who fancied himself to be a conductor. He hired some musicians in order to rehearse and present a concert.

At the first break in the first rehearsal, a percussionist confided to another musician that he didn't think that he could last to the end of the rehearsal because of the ineptness of the conductor. His friend reminded him that they were being well paid for their services and urged him to return to the stage for the rest of the rehearsal.

Fifteen or twenty minutes into the second half, the percussionist had reached the limit of his tolerance and began to hit everything in the percussion department with all possible force. The conductor stopped the orchestra and asked, "*Who did that?*"

Chapter VI

Dull History, Best Forgotten, About Instruments Hard To Ignore

This chapter is mostly about the technical aspects and origins of some of the orchestral instruments, as well as other factors that have influenced the symphony orchestra.

The oboe probably was an import from India. I suspect that an Indian fakir was on tour through the mid-East and then Greece and finally the Italian peninsula, when his snake died. Besides climbing a rope and disappearing, and lying on a bed of nails, he also charmed a snake to come out of a basket as he played on a double reed instrument, later developed into the oboe.

After the snake died, he decided to leave the oboe playing in his act because the sound attracted customers to the end of the market place which was the usual location for his performance. I've been told that snakes are deaf and will only come out of their lair in response to the hypnotic movement of the musician. This activity still seems to be part of the oboe playing tradition.

Anyway, this oboist joined a wandering band of minstrels who played in the streets as an orchestra and collected coins from passersby thus becoming true professional musicians. Unfortunately, the number and kind of instruments in the group have been lost to the music historian, but the oboe came to be accepted as an ensemble instrument and eventually found its way into the orchestra.

Another little known bit of musical trivia is that one of the earliest oboe players on record is also well-known for his involvement in a famous case of betrayal. His name is Judas Iscariot.

You may ask "*How do you know that he played the oboe?*" I will tell you.

The money box in which Judas kept the disciples' funds (You do remember, of course, that he was their treasurer) was a *glossokonon*, which in Greek means a small case for keeping a musician's reeds. Translators of the Bible weren't knowledgeable about reed cases and so translated this Greek word as "box". This may also account for the strange phrase "*having to pay the piper*", even though later folk lore attributes this to the first oboe in the Hamelin Philharmonic.

The oboe has traditionally sounded the note "*A*" before the rehearsal or concert so that all musicians present will tune to the same pitch. The origin of this tradition has never been satisfactorily explained up to the present. Through diligent research I have unearthed the true beginning of this tradition and gladly share it for your edification.

Many ages ago in the dim, misty beginnings of the orchestra, there lived an oboist playing in an orchestra of reasonably high musical achievement and more than local reputation. This oboist suffered under the usual indignities visited on him by the incompetent conductor and an insufferably egotistical concertmaster. Being a fine player both technically and musically, he cast about in his mind for some way to gain the fame and recognition that was his due. He finally formulated a plan that he felt might work, inasmuch as it was based on the knowledge that both the conductor and concertmaster, as well as all other orchestra members (with the exception of the second oboist), were totally ignorant of the technique of oboe playing. After taking the second oboist into his confidence, he proceeded to put his plan to action.

At the next rehearsal, he purposely and consistently played slightly below the pitch of the rest of the orchestra. The other musicians of course noticed this immediately, some adjusting and some stubbornly resisting, with the result that the pitch discrepancies were finally even noticed by the conductor. Not having a clue as to how all this started, he called for a break in rehearsal so that he could confer privately with the concertmaster.

The concertmaster fingered the principal oboist immediately as the cause of the problem and suggested immediate dismissal. This caused a serious problem for the conductor as he was heavily involved with the oboist's lovely young wife (part of the plan) and rightly foresaw a quick ending to a delightful relationship as well as an end to his own continuation on the podium if certain influential people at court learned of this. *What to do?*

The conductor called off the rest of the rehearsal, feigning sudden illness (he didn't have to feign much).

Naturally a private meeting took place between oboist and conductor, certain things were discussed and compromises agreed upon. The conductor announced at the next rehearsal that henceforth, at all rehearsals and performances, the oboist would sound an "*A*" to which all orchestra members would harken attentively and match with their individual tuning and adjustments. He also mumbled a slightly garbled explanation of the need to operate thusly because of the difficulty in carving reeds and making adjustments thereto to accommodate others' pitches. Unfortunately, the latter part of the story is all that has survived and it is untrue because, as anyone knows who has played an oboe, and also other wind instruments, the oboe is the easiest of all winds to alter pitch with the embouchure.

Briefly, the rest of the story is that the oboist's wife remained the mistress of the conductor, and was later elevated to Mrs. Conductor, which was fine with the oboist, as she had been a terrible cook.

Besides, a secret alliance with the tympanist's wife was developing in a most encouraging manner!

The flute started out in the form of what is now called the recorder, sometimes called the fipple flute. This, of course, is played out in front of the face where the performer can see his own fingers and thus keep track of what is going on.

One day some fipple flautist broke his fipple just before a concert at court. Knowing that the penalty for failing to appear at the command performance at court would likely be loss of his own personal fipple, he strove mightily to come up with a quick fix. Being a tippler, as well as a fippler, he remembered that sound could be made by blowing across a bottle. He quickly borrowed a reed knife from the oboe player sitting next to him and began to alter his broken fipple by carving a hole in the top where the air had previously been split to produce the vibrating air column.

Well, of course it didn't work. Then he remembered that a bottle has a closed bottom so he stuffed a rag in the bottom of the flute. What do you know! That didn't work either. By this time he was in a frantic panic as it was almost downbeat time. In complete frustration he hurled his flute to the ground where it imbedded itself, fipple end down. Just then came the downbeat and, as luck would have it, a flute solo was expected only eight bars along. He yanked the instrument from the earth, put the tone hole to his lips and was surprised to find that he could make it work. Enough dirt had stayed in the tube to close the pipe at the correct end for it to play.

This particular fluter, not being too bright, continued many years stuffing dirt in the end of his flute, teaching at the local music academy all about what kind of dirt worked best, stuffing techniques, etc. It has been variously reported that he produced a very learned thesis on the subject and was awarded a doctorate but fortunately it has apparently not survived to the present. Someone else went on to develop the transverse flute which is the present flute style.

Many people, including some horn players, are not aware that the French horn was originally a long straight tube with a small cupped mouthpiece at one end and a flaring bell at the other. You may have seen Alpenhorns which still maintain this form. In France the horn was used to signal to other hunters during the chase of the fox. (As Oscar Wilde put it in reference to the country gentleman galloping after a fox, *"The unspeakable in full pursuit of the inedible."*) In order for this long straight horn to be carried on horseback at the hunt, the services of three mounted musicians were necessary. The foremost *(cloche cheval de chasse)* carried the bell, the midmost *(intermediare cheval de chasse)* the long tube, and the aftermost *(morceau bouche cheval de chasse musicien)* carried the mouthpiece end and blew the corresponding signals to inform the hunters about the progress of the chase.

One fine day, the three musician equestrian hunters were chasing merrily after the fox across the meadows tootling away, when the horse carrying the bell holder stepped in a gopher hole, spilling horse and rider. Because of the necessary proximity of the other mounts and riders, they also fell in a heap. Fortunately, no one of the six, horses plus riders, was seriously injured, but they (the musicians, not the horses) at first were unable to find the horn. The horn players were more addlepated than usual for horn players because of the rapid dismount just suffered, but after a diligent search one of them finally saw that the horn was lying under a bush with its shape much altered. He picked it up and found that it was all coiled up. Thus was the present shape of the horn accidentally invented. It was now called *cor francais de spirale,* later shortened and translated to French horn.

The unfortunate sequel to this tale is that only one man was needed to both play and carry the horn from then on, thus resulting in two men losing employment because of this wonderful accidental technological development. (See earlier note about musicians' union.)

The trombone might never have been invented if castles hadn't had moats and dungeons. You see, the moat water often leaked into the dungeon and had to be removed so that the prisoners, guards, and torture chamber personnel wouldn't drown. For many years prisoners with buckets did the necessary bailing out (Do you suppose that's where the term "bail" came from for prisoners being released?) The guards occasionally lost prisoners on that detail, to say nothing about valuable buckets.

There was one guard who got tired of unlocking cell doors and having to count the prisoners after bail duty and he set out to invent another way to remove the water. He tried many devices: buckets hoisted with pulleys, buckets on an endless rope around two wheels and others, but none was very satisfactory.

One evening while nursing a stein at the local bierhaus, he noticed that the innkeeper used a device with a little handle to bring the liquid from the barrel to the glass. There is no record of how he learned the secret of the little pump, but he did and built himself one to a larger scale that would lift water from the dungeon rooms to the moat.

The next development toward the trombone didn't happen for several years, in fact not before the invention had been duplicated and found its way into almost all castles in the area. Now comes the exciting part of the story.

There was a traveling minstrel named Lassus who was a very good musician and story teller (no relation to Orlando Lassus, another musician of antiquity). One day he appeared at the castle of a prince who was very proud and vain.

One of the funny stories that Lassus used to warm up the court at the beginning of his act, was about a man with a wooden leg. (*"There once was a man with a wooden leg named Charlie."*) Unbeknownst to him was the fact that the prince, before whom he was appearing, had a wooden leg and tried to keep that fact secret from all his subjects. The prince waxed wroth at Lassus' opening joke, had Lassus thrown into the dungeon, and destroyed his lute (predecessor of the electric guitar).

First chair horse and rider
after historic fall

Now if Lassus had been able to have his lute with him, he probably would have been more or less content to sing and polish up his act for whenever he could resume his travels. After all, he was out of the elements, was fed every day, and his bookings had not been all that lucrative lately. However, he felt lost with no instrument, because music was his whole life.

It so happened that the water pump was in his cell, and he inspected it out of curiosity. There was a suction pipe, a discharge pipe, and a handle that worked a pump between them. He partially dismantled it from the wall where it was attached, and found, after much experimenting, that he could blow into one pipe to make a tone and move the handle to produce a different tone. Now he had an instrument to make music and relieve his boredom.

After his release, he developed and refined the instrument, calling it *Wagenschmierpumpe*, and found that he could make a living out of playing in church to accompany the choir in their plainsong. This instrument became known as a *sackbut* in the local dialect where it first became popular, and translated in English was called slush pump. When the instrument finally became known to the Italians, they named it trombone.

Many years later some composer decided to honor the inventor and wrote a piece called *Lassus Trombone*.

One of the first valves that gained a following among brass players was a rotary valve, changing the air stream into a longer passage by turning a quarter turn. The horn still uses this kind of valve as does the bass trombone and many tubas. The piston valve was invented at or near the same time as the rotary, but in a different configuration than used now. The modern piston valve is always used in the trumpet in orchestras in the New World. Many European orchestra trumpet players use rotary valve instruments, so the tradition is different on each side of the Atlantic.

Sometime around the year 1900, horn players began to use a new instrument called a double horn, being pitched in two different keys with a fourth valve to change from one keyed side of the horn to the other. The old hand horn, as the valveless horn was called, was always made with many extra crooks or lengths of pipe that could be inserted to change the fundamental key of the available bugle notes. Composers always wrote the horn parts in the key of "C" with a notation telling the player which keyed crook to use, as stated earlier. Even after the valve horn came into use, composers continued writing this way for years as if they didn't trust that this valve business was here to stay.

The double horn may have been invented to make two different crooks available at the flick of a finger, but really became popular as a practical system of eliminating a section of tubing to make it easier to produce upper register notes with more ease and accuracy.   Double horns were part of the horn tradition by mid-century in the Americas at least. One major orchestra in the USA had a first horn player who was proud of the fact that he was the only one left who still used a single F horn as late as the 1940s.

Thomas Edison's invention of the gramophone has played quite a part in fostering changes in the orchestra. I knew a man who was active in the earliest attempts to record the symphonic orchestra, and he once explained to me how it was done.

All early recordings were made by a vibrating membrane at the small end of a megaphone, attached to a stylus that scratched a wavy line in a waxed cylinder or disc. Sounds very far from the megaphone simply were not recorded, so a special recording studio was constructed for the orchestra. The room was tall enough to stack the orchestra members on scaffolding, but shallow front to back so that all instruments were the shortest possible distance from the recording horn. Instrumentalists with incidental solos left their chairs to rush up to the megaphone and played directly into it. The French horns, because the bell faces away from the audience, were seated facing the back of the room and watched the conductor with the aid of a mirror.

Amazing

Holzernbein Schloss,
birthplace of the trombone

Eventually electronic improvements insured a better product with normal seating of the musicians, but records still had to be recorded non-stop through the entire piece. Because record companies wanted to keep costs down, they wanted as few "takes" as possible, so pressure began to build on the musicians to be perfect every time. (I know of some popular recording artists who would curse loudly into the mike if they heard any wrong notes or playing that they thought was not up to the highest standards, so that the record company wouldn't release the record until a perfect take was made.)

The result of so many perfect records being made and sold, was to impose a much higher standard of performance on all live orchestra concerts. This produced better music performances, but also caused more stress on the musician. Of course the recording technology is so far advanced now that engineers can erase and repair anything that does not suit them or the conductor, because all recording is done on tape instead of a wax disc.

The story is told of a promising young pianist who was engaged to record both Chopin piano concertos with an orchestra. Unfortunately, he was not artistically ready to do justice to the music and there were many breakdowns and retakes at the recording session. Finally the engineers were able to piece together the parts of many different tapes and called the pianist and conductor to the control room to hear the result. After listening to the resultant tape the pianist said, "*Not bad!*" The conductor replied, "*It's very good. Don't you wish that you could play like that?*"

The orchestra developed into its present form due to many influences, but primarily through the ears of musicians who evaluated each potential addition to the ensemble. It is not through luck, but because of the tone, potential expressive possibilities, and the ability to blend with the original string format that determined additions to the orchestra. Lawrence Welk's instrument simply did not pass the test, and there were other instruments that were tried from time to time, even as long ago as Haydn's time, that did not win acceptance.

Chapter VII

Life In An Aural Museum

The symphony orchestra is riddled with tradition, in fact, is little else but tradition! Some refer to the orchestra as a museum for music. The implication is that whatever the orchestra presents is necessarily a representation of times gone by. Of course, all orchestras program contemporary works during the season, but these are received by the audience with feelings similar to those felt when one must take unpleasant tasting medicine. The musicians are rarely elated at finding contemporary works scheduled. There are several reasons why this is so.

The contemporary composer always writes music that is difficult to perform. He or she is out to break new musical ground, so to speak, and the music must be complicated and difficult or it would sound just like some traditional composer of the past. New sounds that haven't been done before take great energy to produce both by the composer and the orchestra members. One contemporary composer told me a reason, that never would have occurred to me, why he makes his music difficult to perform. He wrote a piece that was programmed by one of the major orchestras for performance. The conductor felt that the piece was so easy that he only allotted little more rehearsal time than one playing of the piece before the concert. The composer was disappointed that the musicians had no time to become familiar with the music before playing it for an audience and he felt that his music was poorly presented to the public. He never made the mistake of writing music that was too easy again.

The appearance of the orchestra on stage is certainly traditional. There are a few variations on the arrangement of the sections of the orchestra, but at first glance even to the experienced concert-goer they look the same. Stokowski guest-conducted our orchestra once and he rearranged the instruments on stage in a unique way. He placed all the strings on the left of the stage (as viewed by the audience) and all woodwinds, brass and percussion on the right. I thought that acoustically this made sense because the strings all projected the sound toward the audience to the same advantage. The disadvantage to this was that the strings were very crowded and the others had more than their share of the space. If he had allowed the podium to be placed off center to the right side, this would have worked well. I am sure that an arrangement that removed him from the center of attention was unthinkable.

The dress of the players is another tradition. The white tie and tails are still with us, but not completely. Notice that the female musicians (their presence being another break with tradition) don't wear white tie and tails. I recall a time when the women of the orchestra decided to have a uniform type of clothing that looked much like the men's tie and tails. This lasted one season and was rejected by the ladies as it was uncomfortable and restricted movement. We male musicians had to stay with our traditional full dress.

I have touched on another tradition elsewhere: the oboe sounding the "A" for the musicians to tune. Many orchestras have abandoned this practice since the invention of meters that can read the pitch and give a visual measurement of it, and also the availability of electric tone generators. The story is told of a conductor who insisted that all musicians, before the concert, would go one at a time into a small room where there was an electronic tuning machine and tune to it. All the violin players used the same violin, passing it one to another as they entered and left the room thus destroying the intent of the conductor's edict. Most professional players probably own such a device these days and use it all the time at home so the "A" sounded on stage is no more than a safety check.

We often think of tradition as never changing, but all traditions have a beginning and may change over time. The material used in the manufacture of instruments is traditional but subject to change. We expect that string instruments are made of wood, always were and always will be. There have been string instruments made of aluminum, with a wood grain finish, that were reported to have been used in one particular orchestra until the conductor discovered and put a stop to the practice. The musicians who used them were evidently satisfied with the sound produced and all other aspects of performance, and the conductor didn't learn the truth from his ears.

String players are ever searching for older instruments made by famous makers. It is traditional that all good violinists will play on a Stradivarius or Amati or an instrument made by one of their pupils. In fact all such instruments in use have been rebuilt to withstand the added strain of using steel strings and so probably sound much different now than when first made. There are many fine violin makers currently turning out instruments just as good. I remember reading a paper written by a violin maker not too many years ago. The writer of the paper had access to several famous "name" violins and was able to do much comparison with modern violins both through the use of others' expert ears and also by sound analysis with laboratory instruments. The conclusion was that sometimes the older instruments had slightly better sound because the purfling got loose with age. (*Purfling* is the small strip of wood around the edge of the top and back of the violin designed to inhibit splitting and also for decoration.)

There is a feeling of response that is different for each instrument and every musician is able to recognize this difference as he or she uses the instrument, even though the listener or even sound analysis equipment might indicate no detectable difference in the sound. In simpler terms, some are easier to play than others. I suppose there might well be psychological influences at work in the mind of one playing on a famous expensive instrument.

There is constant controversy among wind instrument players about the proper material that should be used for their various instruments. As of this writing there are traditional correct materials for each instrument, but this has varied over the years. It is easy to condemn an experimental new material because so many different factors enter into the production of a fine instrument, and even the best instrument makers turn out products that vary greatly in playing ease, tone quality and other features.

Before Boehm reworked the flute (See Chapter III.), the instrument was usually made of wood, and continued so for many years. Glass had been tried as well as many different species of wood. Grenadilla became the wood of choice and thus traditional. Eventually silver began to be used for flutes and soon replaced wood. I knew a flute player who bought one of the first silver flutes. He was ostracized by his colleagues so severely that he painted it black to prevent further criticism. Very few, if any, professional players now use a wooden flute. Now the flute tradition seems to be driven by the idea that the material has to be the most expensive to produce the best instrument, having progressed from silver to gold and even platinum. I have even heard that one instrument maker offers a flute with silver on the outside and gold on the inside, two tubes bonded together.

Painting the Flute

Oboes and clarinets are still in the wood tradition even though metal and plastic ones have been manufactured for many years. The metal and plastic oboes and clarinets were made for student use and thus were of low quality, but there is no reason why high quality ones could not be made except that no professional musicians would buy them. Bassoons are made of wood and always have been as far as I know, but bassoonists don't like for others to know that all modern ones are lined with rubber through the first descending section, and of course the bent tube (bocal) that holds the reed is of brass or silver as is the U-shaped part where the direction is reversed at the bottom of the instrument.

We would expect the so-called brass instruments to be made of that material, but there are many alloys that go by the generic term brass, and some instruments are made of an alloy known as German silver which looks like silver instead of brass.

When the brass instruments first came into the orchestra the valve hadn't been invented yet. Haydn and Mozart wrote for brass that could only use the bugle tones although Mozart's horn concertos used other notes made by stopping the bell with the hand. During Beethoven's time the valve was invented and he wrote a part for the fourth horn in his ninth symphony which had to be played on a valve horn. It seems likely that he wrote with a particular orchestra and player in mind.

Another tradition has to do with the makers of the woodwind and brass instruments. For many years only bassoons made by a particular German manufacturer were used in orchestras. Oboes and English horns were made by a certain French instrument maker and the best French horns were of German make. Clarinets were usually from a different French maker than the oboes, and one of the best flute makers was English. The cymbals used by the percussionists were always made by a particular Turkish firm. Perhaps no one else made instruments to their high standards, or there was some other reason why instrumentalists hung on to these biases. These biases are not as pervasive as formerly, now that American manufacturers have successfully entered the market. Sometimes pressure is brought to bear on players to use the same make and model instrument as the section leader, supposedly to ensure unanimity of sound.

A few orchestras specialize in being historically correct by having the musicians use instruments exactly like those used when the music was composed, for there is no doubt that when a modern orchestra plays Mozart, the sound is not at all as it would have been heard by Mozart himself.

All the old violins have been altered in many ways and most importantly use steel strings under more tension than was the case in Haydn's day, so the sound is louder and of different quality. The flutes are now made with a straight bore instead of tapered, and have many more keys with larger tone holes to allow the sound to be more full. The horns and trumpets now use valves, so we see that some of the traditions evolve and change over the years.

The tone quality of each instrument in the orchestra is traditional, but there have been changes even here over the years. One factor that probably had some effect in this regard was the size of concert halls. Another was the size of the orchestra itself. Still the tradition of whether or not to use vibrato on certain instruments rarely changes. The strings always are played with vibrato (except the harp of course) as are flutes, oboes and bassoons, but the application of vibrato has changed over the years. There was a time when violins only used vibrato for emphasis on long notes much as a trill might be employed now. In symphonic work the clarinet and all the brass are played without vibrato. I do remember that one first horn on a recording made by a major orchestra used a slight vibrato at times. (Maybe he was uncomfortable at recording sessions and I don't blame him.)

The tone quality of the French horn seems to have gone through a major change in the last twenty years or more. I am uncomfortable with words used to describe tone quality as they are so imprecise. However, I shall try to convey the differences that I hear. If the reader is familiar with band music, you may recall what a baritone horn sounds like. There was a time when the French horn had a light fluffy, though centered, sound with a soft kind of attack, or beginning, to the note. I think that larger orchestras and concert halls have forced horn players to change to larger bore instruments and also to use the Bb side of the instrument lower than sounds proper, with the result that the sound is now very close to the baritone horn sound.

I have noted elsewhere that the horn is fingered with the left hand even though most players are right-handed. Tradition dictates that each instrument is held and manipulated the same way whether one is right- or left-handed, although I know of a few instances where this tradition has been challenged. I knew a trombone player who assembled his instrument so that he could maneuver the slide with the left hand, and a trumpet player who manipulated the valves with the fingers of his left hand, but in both cases most observers would not notice the difference.

A violinist trying to play left-handed would need to have an instrument extensively altered because reversing the order of the strings also changes the way that the strongest tensions are transferred to the body of the instrument. Also, try to visualize how the player would be handicapped in trying to fit into the section with the others. Interestingly, I hear that it has been done!

There are some other traditions less apparent to the casual concert attender. String players traditionally share music with two players to each music stand. These are designated as outside and inside players with the outside player being the one closest to the audience. When pages need to be turned it is always the inside player who turns while the outside player continues to play. I have been told that when the Japanese first began to have symphony orchestras in the Western style it created a problem in the string sections because of a cultural bias that would not allow the outside player to continue playing as his partner stopped to turn the page. Thus the whole string section ceased to produce music at each page turn.

One other tradition that is not likely to be apparent to the concert-goer has to do with the relationships between the musicians in the different sections. Almost universally, string players feel that they work harder than the winds and percussion and so should be paid more. Wind players frequently remind the strings that sometimes one note might be more difficult to produce than a complete page of violin music. This rivalry is usually carried on in a friendly manner, but I recall once when the concertmaster was stung by a verbal barb hurled his way by one member of the horn section and replied that he thought that he would take a week off from the violin and learn the horn.

It is quite possible that I have failed to mention some aspects of the orchestra that are traditional, because I was so much involved for so long that many orchestral procedures seemed the only correct way, and thus escaped my notice as being the result of tradition.

I think that if I had stayed with the music business longer, I might have tried to change or add some new traditions to the institution. On second thought, maybe there are too many traditions already.

Chapter VIII

A Funny Thing Happened On The Way To The Concert

Every profession, job or hobby has jokes that only have meaning to those engaged in those particular pursuits. Such stories are often incomprehensible or lacking in humor to outsiders. As an example, surgeons and dentists probably have experiences that will have their colleagues rolling on the floor with uncontrolled paroxysms of jollity when regaled with them at their conventions, but I probably wouldn't find them funny and, furthermore, don't even want to hear them. In other words, this chapter may only be of interest to musicians and might prove to be puzzling to others.

All of the following stories are assumed to be true. I was personal witness to some, but most were passed on from friends and acquaintances as having been observed by them. Such stories must, of course, be suspect but may still be worth passing on. A third category will be added at the end of this chapter which may have happened, but may only be apocryphal as they are told about different orchestra players and conductors. No orchestras or people are identified, with one exception, in order to protect the guilty. None of these stories are identified as my favorites and many will not seem to be worth writing down, but one never knows what experiences a reader might have had that may seem similar and thus elicit a chuckle.

Sir Thomas Beecham is the one person I wish to identify because his wit and personality are unique and many stories about him would be unthinkable as being true of anyone else.

Sir Thomas was conducting *Oberon Overture* at a post-season concert out of town with no rehearsal, but it had been performed early in the season. All orchestra members were so familiar with it that this seemed perfectly natural until they were seated on stage awaiting Sir Thomas' entrance. One of the first violins, noticing the adagio sostenuto and remembering the exposed con sordino (muted) passage in the second measure, started asking around whether the maestro conducted that in four or in eight. The first measure is played by the first horn alone and is traditionally not conducted so gives no clue. No one could remember and now everyone who had been asked began to worry. A second desk player poked the concertmaster in the back with his bow and asked him. The concertmaster was suddenly worried about a possible impending disaster and now Sir Thomas was coming on stage. The concertmaster got the eye of the maestro and managed to mouth out the necessary query. Sir Thomas stroked his goatee made no reply and cued the horn to begin. There were no problems with the second measure and the story teller (the concertmaster) in relating the story still couldn't remember if Sir Thomas conducted those measures in four or in eight.

Again under Beecham the orchestra was in the second half of the final rehearsal before the concert when the concertmaster realized that there was a Mozart symphony in the folder for that evening's concert that the orchestra had not rehearsed yet. At the very next opportunity he apprised Sir Thomas of that fact.

Sir Thomas replied, "*I know how it goes.*"

It was performed at the concert without rehearsal.

An additional version, that may or may not be related to that incident, is that there was a young first season second violinist who observed to the maestro that he never had played that particular Mozart symphony before and was naturally disturbed at the prospect of no rehearsal.

Sir Thomas: *"You'll love it."*

In his declining years he guest conducted a concert in which I played. At the rehearsal a high stool with backrest and arms was on the podium for his use. He was ushered in and introduced to the orchestra by a female member of the management staff. After the introduction Sir Thomas got up on the podium and then the stool with a little difficulty. The management lady was obviously alarmed for his safety and said, *"Is it too high, Sir Thomas?"*

His reply: *"Only physically!"*

It has been reported that he once observed, *"The English people don't really like music, but they thoroughly love the noise that it makes!"*

There was a lovely old gentleman who played the English horn so musically and beautifully that a famous guest conductor during rehearsal stopped the orchestra, immediately after an English horn solo, stepped off the podium, shook his hand, expressed his pleasure, and asked about his teachers and experience. The next season the orchestra was rehearsing *El Amor Brujo* which has a prominent English horn solo. The resident conductor was unhappy with the result and kept after the player to make it more excited and wild in sound. The conductor finally said to the old gentleman, *"You have to imagine that you're making love to a beautiful Spanish senorita!"*

The reply: *"Oh! I thought it was a bullfight!"*

At the end of the season the English horn player resigned from the orchestra, sold his instruments and never played again.

Sometimes instrumentalists continue to play long past their prime, often because not all orchestras have adequate retirement plans. There were two elderly gentlemen flute players sitting in first and second chairs. The first player was losing his hearing and the second had very poor eyes and wore extremely thick glasses. The conductor had stopped the orchestra at rehearsal to make some suggestion or other, and it was apparent that rehearsal was to continue.

First flute player sotto voce to second flute: *"What did he say?"*

Second flute player also sotto voce: *"He said to start at letter B. Where is it?"*

In the same orchestra the first oboe sat between the principal flute and the second oboe who also was slightly hard of hearing. From time to time a musician might need to communicate to another, and this is only done in emergencies, and very discreetly. In concert the first oboe player lost the count in a long pianissimo string passage, and began to panic as he realized that he could not ask for any help from those on either side without being heard over the soft string sounds, because the only two players close enough would not hear him unless he raised his voice. He had to rely on instinct to play at the proper place.

Those with no orchestral experience may find it hard to believe that a musician could lose his or her place in the music during performance. I remember a concert that I was part of where a well known concert violinist got lost in the middle of the first movement of a concerto that he had probably played a hundred times or more. Who knows what caused this lapse: simple loss of memory, attention diverted somehow, anticipation of an interesting invitation tendered just before the concert, or what? The point is that if a world-class concert violinist can have it happen, then we run-of-the-mill symphony players can become lost, and no doubt will, if in the profession long enough. Usually the player will be able to find his way again without any outside help, but occasionally panic takes over and assistance is needed RIGHT NOW!

The orchestra came to a place in the music where there was a short but sustained silence intended. This was interrupted in the concert by a frantic voice in the viola section:

"Where the ---- are we?!!"

Another time, in rehearsal of an extremely fast and difficult piece, a first violinist in the rear where it is difficult to see the conductor, asked imploringly, *"Forget the rehearsal letters. What page are we on?".*

Sometimes the music itself can be of such a nature that the mind has difficulty in keeping alert as in the following story.

Wagner's *Overture to Tannhauser* has a violin part that is very repetitious with a descending figure in a scotch snap kind of rhythm (short note long note). A violinist in the orchestra told me once that he dreamt that he was playing *Tannhauser* and when he awoke he found that he was!

A traveling ballet company was doing *Swan Lake* in a small midwestern city. Just before the first performance, the percussionist became ill and was rushed to the hospital. Hurried phone calls by the contractor finally located the only available drummer in town whose experience was primarily playing the local vaudeville house many years before. He rushed to the theater and into the pit just in time for the downbeat.

After the first ballet the conductor whispered to the contractor, *"Get him out of here, we'll do without percussion!"*

"What's wrong", said the amazed drummer. *"I caught everything!"* (In vaudeville loud snare drum rim shots are common emphasis for leaps, falls, etc.)

An opera company traveled from the United States to Canada to perform, and the buses with the orchestra aboard were detained at the border by the customs officials. The performance was to be in a movie theater built during vaudeville days with a pit of sufficient size for the orchestra, but the conductor would enter from a side aisle and conduct from outside the orchestra pit rail. Word never got to the conductor that the orchestra had not arrived at curtain time so he made his way out the aisle, bowed to acknowledge the applause and was surprised when he turned with baton upraised to find that a downbeat would be wasted on an empty orchestra pit. He had to make an embarrassing exit and await the arrival of the musicians.

The same opera company was traveling with two operas prepared, including scenery and costumes for both. The second opera was to be performed the second night in a city reached by ferry. The scenery, costumes and orchestra music for the first one were sent back to the home city after the first performance. The orchestra members assembled in the pit the following night to find that the music on their stands was for the wrong opera and that the correct parts were on the truck headed home. The opera performance was delayed to the next evening and the parts were retrieved in time.

A different opera company this time, but the performance was again in a theater that had been built for vaudeville. In the back wall of the pit was a large electrical box that had been used at one time to allow the vaudeville conductor to have control over lighting. One of the French horn players found himself sitting uncomfortably close to this closed box because of the crowded pit. Things went well until along in the second act when the horn player had to quickly pull a slide on his horn to empty the accumulated moisture. In doing so he inadvertently hit the box with his shoulder. Instantly every light in the theater went out and stayed out. It took the electricians ten minutes or more to jury-rig the back stage panels and get lights so that the performance could continue. The horn player didn't tell anyone what caused the blackout until later.

Again a traveling opera company was playing in the same kind of theater doing Faust. In the scene where the heroine is outside the cathedral in reverent contemplation, she is supposed to be deeply moved by the music of the choir and organ coming from the church. A small electric organ was ready backstage and a microphone was in place for the small chorus representing the church choir. In the rush of the chorus getting in place, the extension cord to the organ was accidentally disconnected, and this was not noticed by anyone. Unfortunately, the chorus mike was still live, so when the downbeat was given for the chorus to start there was a delay of a second or two and then came the highly amplified voice of the organist: *"Who pulled the damn plug!?"*.

There was a first violinist who was known throughout the orchestra for his eccentric behavior. His ability was not in question, he was assistant concertmaster at one time, and also had been a member of Johann Strauss' orchestra in Vienna. As time went on he was moved back one stand each year, mostly because guest conductors found his behavior disturbing and complained to the management.

One time at rehearsal the conductor kept having the first violins repeat over and over the same passage because he was not happy with the beginning attack and energy expended. One more attempt was asked for and the rest of the orchestra was treated to the sight of all the violins prepared to do their best with bow at the frog (for maximum volume) firmly planted on the string, all except our friend, who was sitting up extra straight and erect with bow arm straight up in the air ready to flail the hell out of his poor violin. In similar circumstances another time, he asked if the conductor would like for him to frown.

One year he was assigned a stand partner not to his liking and decided to take action. All players count to themselves during rests, but in the string sections where everyone plays together it is not a serious problem. If you lose count you just get ready and start with the others. As the time approached at the end of a long rest, our man put his violin up a little early. This caused his stand partner to lose confidence in the count and to also prepare to play. One measure before the proper entrance he made a pronounced downward motion as if starting to play and the poor partner made a loud solo entrance at the wrong place. After the concert the unfortunate soloist complained loudly to the personnel manager and conductor. At the next rehearsal seating arrangements were adjusted so that both had new stand partners.

My orchestral experiences all took place in the United States and Canada. I understand that across the Atlantic some things may be different. For instance, I have been told that what we call the intermission is known in Britain as "*The Interval*" and that, furthermore, the English musician always enjoys a pint of some mildly alcoholic beverage during the interval, which habit would be a serious infraction of the union rules on this side of the ocean.

In a European orchestra one of the viola players had reached retirement age. At his final rehearsal the orchestra members had a party for him during the interval, and the conductor suggested that he need not play the rest of the rehearsal but might use the time to remove his personal possessions from his locker and go home early which he gratefully did.

When he arrived home his dear wife was out working in the garden and was curious about his early unexpected arrival. He explained about the party at which his colleagues very kindly honored him for his many years of faithful service and that the conductor had let him leave early.

She replied, *"Oh, how lovely, but what is it that you have under your arm?"*

"This is my viola," he answered.

"Oh, yes," she replied, *"I have heard you speak of it."*

In doing some research many years ago I read the history of all the major symphony orchestras in the United States and ran across accounts in two orchestra histories that I think may be related. One of the orchestras on the Eastern Seaboard fired a 'cellist, even though he was a competent musician, because he refused to share music with anyone. (All string players read two people to each stand of music.)

American musicians backstage at intermission.
European musicians would have some alcoholic beverage in
hand for the same scene.

The following year an orchestra on the West Coast offered a contract to a 'cellist who won an audition, but it was noted that he had a peculiar disability. He was only able to read music upside down. I suspect that it was the same man who creatively made sure that he would never have to share music with anyone.

Several of the symphony musicians in a large midwestern city had employment at the local radio station on Saturday each week for a broadcast designed for the entertainment and information of the farmers throughout the country. Near the end of the program there was always a break for the orchestra while farm commodity prices were read and comment made thereon. The musicians of course paid no attention, but talked freely among themselves as the studio mikes were not live during the announcements. Normal procedure had always been that the orchestra played two numbers after the reports, a waltz followed by a march to finish.

One day the market reporting segment went on longer than usual, and even the conductor was caught off guard until the red light lit up indicating that the mikes were now live in the studio. One glance at the clock by the conductor and he knew that there was time for only one piece, so he quickly picked up the score of the waltz, turned it over in view of all the musicians, or so he thought, and opened the score of the march followed within seconds by the downbeat. Only about half of the musicians had been alert or astute enough to note what the conductor had tried to convey in sign language, so half the orchestra played the march and half started the waltz. The conductor looked desperately toward the control booth, made a slashing motion across his throat and the engineer in the booth killed the mikes.

The conductor cut off the orchestra, shouted   *"No, No! The other one!"*

The red light came on, and the down beat produced again the same waltz-march in a new arrangement as each musician followed directions to play "the other one" rather than the one he had started with first.

The orchestra was doing an only rehearsal for an ice-skating extravaganza. Rehearsal time was limited, so much of the music was only begun to show tempo and style, and stopped after a few measures. The conductor stopped the orchestra after the concertmaster had just stumbled, sight reading through a tricky solo. The violinist was dismayed when it became apparent that the conductor intended to go on to the next musical number without giving him another shot at the solo part.

Elderly violinist: "*Can't we run that one down again?*"

Conductor: "*There is a loud announcement of the next act over the PA at that point, and mother will never hear you!*"

The symphony orchestra was rehearsing *Beethoven's Ninth Symphony* in which the fourth horn part has a prominent solo. (See Chapter VII.) The conductor stopped and, addressing the first horn by name, began to give elaborate directions how the solo should be phrased. Finally it was pointed out to the conductor, by the fourth horn player, that the solo was in his part. The conductor then had to justify his error by insisting that it was traditional that the first horn always played that particular part and further directed that it would be performed by the first horn.

In another chapter I wrote of amateur and semi-professional orchestras. Sometimes either of these groups might hire a player from a nearby professional organization to fill in where there is a vacancy that needs to be covered for a concert. In just such a case a clarinetist was engaged to be first chair in an orchestra where the conductor was also a composer. His composition had an important clarinet solo after a short orchestral introduction. The composer-conductor went to great pains to convey to the clarinetist the scene that this solo part was depicting. I believe that a bucolic setting was described with grazing cows, red barn, flowing stream, distant mountains, typical farm buildings, etc.

The orchestra began and at the proper time the conductor attempted to cue the clarinetist who seemed to be hiding behind the music stand with his face in his hands and the clarinet in his lap. The conductor stopped the orchestra.

"*Why didn't you play?*" he asked.

"I couldn't," was the reply, *"I forgot the story!"*

In all orchestras, I am sure, there are groups that become good friends and frequently go out for dinner after the concerts. I was part of such a gathering, because I seldom ate very much before playing. I have many fond memories of those after-concert dinners.

There was a very special group in one orchestra made up of four or five players from different sections. Each time that they went to a post-concert dinner, one of them had his meal paid for by all the others. The honor was won by winning the most points at the rehearsals leading up to that particular concert. One of the members in the percussion section kept score. Points were made by asking the conductor questions during the rehearsal. Simple questions, such as, *"What is the order of the program?"* were worth one point. Questions that required the conductor to refer to the score, such as, *"What is the correct note for the third horn on beat four in measure forty seven?"* were worth two points. Any question which could get the conductor to leave the podium to refer to or inspect the player's part was worth a greater number of points. The player earning the most points during the rehearsals for the concert won the free meal.

There were two viola players sharing a stand, who were easily distracted by any events in the orchestra that seemed humorous to them. During a concert they turned the page only to discover that the next page needed was missing. They both started to giggle and were in full uncontrolled laughter long before the orchestra got to where they again had music to read. The conductor was not amused.

I mentioned earlier that there are some orchestra stories that may or may not be true or that are difficult to authenticate. The first one that comes to mind is told again about Sir Thomas Beecham.

He was engaged to direct *Carmen* by a major opera company. Evidently the opera had been rehearsed and performed recently, so Sir Thomas was to lead one rehearsal and performance. The orchestra and full cast were ready for rehearsal to begin at the appointed time, but there was no evidence of Beecham. Ten minutes later Sir Thomas was seen coming down the aisle of the opera house. He took off his coat and hat, laid them on a seat, entered the pit, and greeted the orchestra.

He then turned to the concertmaster and asked, *"What opera are we doing?"*

"Carmen, Sir Thomas," was the reply.

"Oh, hell," replied Sir Thomas, *"everybody knows Carmen. I'll see you this evening."*

He left the pit, put his coat and hat on and strolled out of the theater.

A well known conductor had an orchestra that was pretty much in awe of him with the exception of the first oboe player who had been in the same conservatory as a classmate back in Italy. The conductor was going on at some length explaining how he wanted a particular oboe solo phrased.

The oboist finally had reached the end of his tolerance, stood up, shook his instrument at the conductor and said, *"What do you want, loud or soft?"*

Oberon Overture was to be conducted by a guest conductor. The first measure is played by the first horn alone, as mentioned earlier. The notes in this first measure are a dotted quarter note, an eighth note, and a half note marked with a fermata (to be held longer at the player's discretion). These are in ascending order scale-wise starting on the tonic.

The conductor told the first horn, *"You've played this many times, so there is no need to rehearse the first measure. Just play it as you think it should be."*

At the concert the first horn played the correct notes except he shortened the time to a dotted sixteenth note followed by a thirty-second note and a staccato eighth note.

The orchestra was to go on a one week tour. The third trumpet player asked the personnel manager if his services would be needed.

The personnel manager checked with the conductor who assured him that there was one piece scheduled that used third trumpet.

At the first city the trumpeter arrived at the theater, and found that the program for that evening did not include the piece for which he was needed. This was the case at every engagement on the tour until the last stop.

Finally he dressed in his tux, carried his instrument to the theater and proceeded to his place on the stage. As the orchestra played *"his piece"* he lost his place in counting the long rest before his entrance and consequently did not play a single note.

At home again he assured his family that the tour had been great fun.

A first oboe player had the reputation of talking out when it would have been best to remain silent. One time at rehearsal he became impatient at the conductor's lengthy explanations and burst out with, *"Maestro, you talk too much!"* The conductor left the podium in a huff and went to his room.

The oboist proceeded to swab out his instrument in preparation to go home as the personnel manager pleaded with him to go and apologize. He finally and reluctantly offered to make the apology, and made his way to the dressing room and knocked on the door.

On being invited to enter he opened the door and said, *"Maestro, I offer you my apology. I am sorry you talk too much!"*

One of the unwritten rules of orchestral behavior is that you don't compliment a colleague on a solo passage well done, until after the last performance of that piece. The following illustrates why.

An orchestra was touring and opened each performance with Rossini's Overture to *The Thieving Magpie* which begins with a snare drum roll starting pianissimo and slowly building to fortissimo. The conductor was so impressed with how well the drummer did this to perfection each night, that he called him into his dressing room just before the next concert, and told him that he had never in all his years of conducting, and before that playing in orchestras, experienced such a superbly controlled crescendo drum roll.

The orchestra assembled on stage and tuned up, the conductor made his entrance, bowed to applause, mounted the podium, and signaled to the drummer to begin. The poor drummer was unable to make his hands function at all, and another drummer had to take the sticks away from him and play the opening roll.

There was an elderly, white-haired man who played percussion in another orchestra. He was assigned to the snare drum by the head percussionist, but the conductor was unhappy with the performance of the part. After four or five times in one rehearsal in which the conductor stopped to make changes or corrections in the snare drum part, the elderly drummer's patience had worn thin. Once more the rehearsal was interrupted, and the conductor again started to address the hapless drummer. Before he could say anything the drummer spoke up.

Elderly drummer: *"Maestro, if you don't like my playing you can just get yourself another boy!"*, and he walked out.

Humorous stories often revolve around guest conductors, because the relationship between musician and leader is fraught with less danger for the musician as the conductor may never be encountered again and also has no authority to terminate a player.

Following are some musician jokes that may or may not have a relationship to real events.

The guest conductor started the first rehearsal with a Brahms symphony, and couldn't help but notice that a man right close to him in the first violins was scowling and grimacing constantly, as he played, as if in pain.

The conductor addressed him, *"It seems plain to me that you don't like Brahms."*

The violinist replied, *"No, no, that's not true! You don't understand. I just don't like music!"*

Professional musicians seldom miss a rehearsal or concert even when seriously ill and so the following story must be about a semi-professional group where members earned their living at other pursuits.

The guest conductor was irritated because there were musicians missing at each rehearsal. At the end of the final rehearsal he spoke to the orchestra.

"I wish to offer my thanks to this fine gentleman in the first violins who appears to me to be the only member who attended all the rehearsals."

Violinist: *"I thought it was the least that I could do as I won't be able to be at the concert tonight."*

A violinist member of the orchestra was in the hospital with a serious illness. Finally he was informed by his doctor that his chances of recovery were remote and that he would never return to the orchestra. Shortly after receiving this news, the conductor showed up at his bedside to visit him. The conductor was quite universally disliked by the members of the orchestra, so the ill violinist thought that he could say things that many felt but only someone in his position could say. He then proceeded to outline every bit of negative feeling including references to the conductor's ancestry and lack of musical integrity and ability.

A few days after this venomous, vituperative conversation, the violinist started a miraculous recovery. In a few weeks, because he still was under contract to play, he was back in the section under the baton of the same conductor.

Sometimes members of one family study the same instrument. There were three brothers in the horn section of one well-known orchestra. Brahms' brother was a pianist and, of course, not as famous as the composer. When he showed up at a gig, he was referred to as *"the wrong Brahms"*.

There was a famous three generation family of horn players in England who all appeared at the same rehearsal one day and some other musician seeing them enter the hall together said, *"Here comes the father, the son, and the holy ghost."*

I will end this chapter with a personal story that was not amusing. I was sitting in the first horn position and directly behind me on a higher level was a stand of the contrabass section. During a concert, I was counting rests before an approaching incidental solo for the horn. I heard some object drop to the floor behind me and thought that one of the players behind me had dropped his rosin. I quickly glanced over my shoulder and saw a bow lying on the floor. Looking up I was horrified to see that the man directly behind me had fainted and was rapidly falling toward me. I stood up and holding my horn in my left hand, put my right hand in the center of his chest to prevent him from falling on me. His stand partner had by this time put his own bass on the floor and grabbed the faintee's bass and proceeded to put it in a safe place. Meanwhile my burden was getting heavier as his knees started to buckle, and my solo was getting closer. Fortunately his stand partner was able to ease his colleague to the floor, and I regained my seat about one beat before the start of my solo.

This was the first time that I had ever played in this orchestra. I had been hired as fourth horn and only was in the first chair position due to the illness of the regular first chair player who had been in that position for many years. My wife had given birth to our first child just hours before this event, so that was a week to remember!

Chapter IX

Life Behind The Music Stand

I recall that once Jack Benny came to do a concert with us as a benefit for the orchestra sustaining fund. As we rehearsed, the resident conductor tried to get Mr. Benny to change one of his routines to make it "funnier". I was appalled at the arrogance of anyone trying to suggest to a comedian of Benny's masterful timing and obvious success and experience, that his performance could be improved. Mr. Benny was most gracious and simply said, *"It'll be all right this way."* If I had been Mr. Benny I would have been tempted to hit the conductor over the head with my famous 150 dollar Stradivarius.

I was lucky enough to have played under Sir Thomas Beecham's baton a few times. His remarks to newspaper reporters and critics were often harsh and scathing, but the times that I sat in the orchestra under his direction, he was generous and kindly in his approach to the musicians. He once got tired of conducting at an afternoon concert being presented in the inner city and turned around to talk to the audience.

As well as I can remember this is what he said:

"When I first started to conduct orchestras, I used to revel in the applause. I accepted the fact that I had done something grand in leading the musicians and creating enjoyment for the listeners.

"But one day, after the applause had died down, I heard a small boy in the front row ask his mother, 'What was he bowing for? He didn't do anything!' and I realized that he was correct.

"The symphonic musical group that you see here is a valuable cultural part of your community and deserves your full loyal support. You support your library and museums with tax dollars as well as with private funds, and this symphony orchestra is just as important to the cultural health of the community as those worthy institutions."

He then went on to tell about how he rehearsed an orchestra.

"Most conductors at rehearsal stop the orchestra when they think that they have heard someone play a wrong note. I never do that because it is such a waste of time. First you have to spend time trying to figure out who might have done it, and then you must figure out a convenient place to begin again, when the fact is that whoever made the error will never ever do it again if he or she can possibly avoid it."

Throughout the previous pages I have been hard on the conducting arm of our profession (a little humor there). I see no reason to name those who were abusive, inept, excessively egotistical, etc., but I do wish to single out some who showed positive qualities that were rare in appearance. One problem in pursuing a course of listing names is that I am extremely aware that I may just be name dropping and not contributing anything of value or interest to these pages. I did have the opportunity of playing under the baton of many famous men, and I am grateful for the honor of that experience.

One season we were without a resident conductor and so had guest conductors for all concerts. We also had less than ideal rehearsal facilities. Maurice Abravanel was rehearsing us and workmen were putting up chairs at the other end of the hall for some event for that evening. The noise was extremely annoying.

Mr. Abravanel, referring to the noise, said to the concertmaster, *"Has this happened before?"*

Concertmaster: *"Every time we rehearse here."*

Mr. Abravanel: *"Has anybody asked them to stop?"*

Concertmaster: *"I don't think so."*

Mr. Abravanel then left the podium, approached the workmen and had a conversation with them which we were unable to hear. He then came back to the podium and resumed rehearsal. The workmen left and there was no more disturbance. He had simply asked them nicely if they could do some other work until we were finished.

Now the reason that I considered this unusual was that all previous conductors in the same situation shouted and made a great fuss from the podium to the workmen with no effect.

Abravanel did something else that left a lasting impression with me. Most times when the orchestra is to accompany a soloist, the first reading through the music is done with the soloist present and playing with us. Abravanel rehearsed the orchestra parts in the rehearsal previous to the appearance of the soloist with an explanation to the effect that it is not only good manners to do our best work when accompanying, but it is our duty to do so.

Another time with a different orchestra William Steinberg was rehearsing for the world premier of Ralph Vaughan Williams' last symphony. There were parts for three saxophones, and players had been hired from the union hall to play the parts. It seemed apparent that they had no previous symphonic experience and they were ill-at-ease. The rehearsal was not going very well until Steinberg made a speech to the sax players to this effect.

"It is obvious to me that you are very capable musicians, but are uncomfortable in this situation and are worried about the outcome. Please do

not be concerned and anxious. I know that you are going to do your parts very well and that the concert will be a huge success."

I remember this so vividly because so many conductors would have created a no-win situation in similar circumstances by brow-beating or demeaning the men.

One of the conductors that I remember with much pleasure was Carlos Chavez. I remember our first rehearsal with him. We played a Haydn symphony through from beginning to end with no stops and no comments. I was appalled that he seemed oblivious to the many places in the music where attention was needed, but then we spent the rest of rehearsal until break time on the introduction to the first movement. He was exacting and demanding but always correct. I heard that a music critic once asked him why he used a score when conducting his own compositions.

He replied, *"Because I know how to read music!"*

Another conductor that merited respect was Emerson Buckley. I played in the opera orchestra several times when he conducted and I am sure that we could have played an opera without rehearsal with him on the podium, with no problems. He not only cued all singers on stage, but all solo parts in the orchestra as well.

Paul Kletski endeared himself to the orchestra as a guest conductor because of his willingness to acknowledge the able musicianship of the orchestral members. I have already conveyed the respect and pleasure we felt when working with Sir Thomas Beecham.

Most symphony concerts have a soloist featured and they are usually well-known musical celebrities. One soloist was not known to me before we began rehearsal, but once I heard her sing, I was so impressed with the way she used her voice that I have never forgotten it. I am not sure whether or not Rita Streich concertized much in the United States, as I never had the privilege of hearing her again, but I cannot recall ever hearing such wonderful control of the human voice, even though I played for many other world-famous singers.

One aspect of orchestra performance that most concert-goers never think about is the printed page that each musician reads as he or she contributes sound to the ensemble. Most well-established orchestras have their own library of all the standard repertoire. There are rental libraries that can furnish complete orchestration parts for almost any symphonic arrangement. Some traveling soloists, especially singers, might furnish their own music containing all their special instructions. Some publishers own the copyrights to particular compositions, allowing no other copies to be printed, so that the orchestration must be rented from them.

Most traveling shows such as the Ice Follies, popular singers, Broadway musicals, etc., carry their own books for each instrument in manuscript form, and don't allow the players to remove them from the theater for practicing. Many times the musicians must come early to the performance to sit in the pit and work through the difficult spots to be ready. Those who arrange and write such music are aware that the abilities of the musicians in each city will vary and so usually avoid writing parts that are too challenging, but all who have played such engagements for several years will someday find a real challenge on the music stand in front of them without adequate time to do complete preparation. This is where all the time at home practicing difficult exercises will pay off.

It seems to be a tradition that traveling ballet companies never have legible music for the musicians to read. Much of the rehearsal is taken up with trying to explain what would be apparent if they furnished legible parts easy to read. Despite this problem, ballet jobs were my favorite, partly because there was almost always a very elegant approach to the music, and especially to the rhythm.

There are rules about the use of rental music that the musicians are supposed to observe. At rehearsal all musicians will have a pencil to put in appropriate reminders about details easily missed during the pressure of performance. All these marks must be erased before the music is returned, but a curious traditional exception has evolved in which many users of the music will sign and date the copy that they use. This usually involves the first chair players who may be familiar with the names of their counterparts in other orchestras.

In the orchestra in which I served there had been a first chair clarinet player who found this habit offensive and often expressed dismay to his colleagues when confronted with music so defaced. One day he was especially outraged at the many signatures in the music before him, took his pencil and wrote, *"Anyone who signs his name to this music is a damn fool!"* For validation, he signed his own name.

In another chapter I wrote about contemporary music. Henry Pleasants wrote a book called *The Agony Of Modern Music,* in which he states,

"What we know as modern music is the noise made by deluded speculators picking through the slag pile".

One colleague of mine often said about such compositions that it's like any other music except for a little hiccup once in awhile.

One time we had just finished a modern piece that had no recognizable melody, form, chord structure or anything at all for a traditionalist to relate to, and as we stood to acknowledge applause, the man next to me remarked, *"Boy! They'll be whistling that one all the way home!"*

I recall another time when we were rehearsing a contemporary piece in which the composer changed the basic time structure sometimes for each successive measure. This made it extremely difficult, especially since the conductor was not noted for his ability to direct time changes. The music was not difficult or complicated, but the way it was written imposed a hardship on the player. A colleague nearby offered the comment, *"If this guy had written the Star-Spangled Banner, I couldn't play it."*

There was one passage that the horn section was having difficulty in playing exactly together. I recognized that the sounds were really quite easy to play and that the constant time changes created the possibility for confusion. I took all the horn parts home and rewrote that passage in four-four time with accents. At the next rehearsal I distributed these insert manuscript parts to the section and suggested that they not watch the conductor, but just play from the new parts. I think that most of them took my suggestion and the passage was no problem anymore.

In this chapter I have tried to undo some of the damage that I may have wreaked on the conducting profession in other parts of this writing, and to relate some experiences with new music. We have to remember that everything we play was new at one time.

During the first performance in this country of Richard Strauss' *Death And Transfiguration,* A lady got up from her seat, strode purposely up the aisle and tossed back over her shoulder: *"I hope that when my time comes, there won't be so much brass!"*

CODA

When I began this soliloquy, I just intended to have some fun remembering and speculating on my own experiences in the symphonic music industry. From an early age I wanted to be a player in a large orchestra. My heroes were the first chair players in the famous orchestras. The illness of the local, very competent, principal player put me into the first horn position of a professional orchestra and I continued in that position for many years.

Because I was first horn for the symphony, contractors for other musical work called me and thus I had the grand experience of playing in several different opera companies as well as ballet, traveling and local productions of Broadway musicals, and working for many celebrated stars traveling through our city. I was also fortunate enough to be engaged in musical work with a fine orchestra in another city a few hours away.

After several years of very interesting musical experiences, I decided to leave the orchestra and pursue another line of work that seemed to offer more financial security. I was also influenced by what might be termed *"working conditions"*, but my work was never challenged by a conductor as was that of some others that I knew.

Symphony musicians are highly skilled and dedicated workers, and thus deserve the respect and recognition of their worth by their employers. Good managers in any field of industry recognize the benefits of treating personnel in ways that may not even cost any money but will enhance the morale of the employee. It should be apparent to symphony managers that this is even more important in dealing with musicians, as they could never be of symphony caliber without an ego that says, *"I am a good performer on my instrument and I insist that you listen!"* In fact, that commanding presence is one of the first things that any audition committee should take note of, as well as technique, intonation, etc.

Symphony orchestra playing is one of the most demanding jobs in the world. Each instrumentalist has to have complete mastery of all aspects of the chosen instrument. Even then there are many fine musicians who never master the art of being one with the large ensemble. Every experienced string player has had a stand partner sometime in his career who, for one reason or another, was difficult to play next to, and spoiled all the fun.

One cannot do the job well unless almost totally immersed in the process. No variation is allowable from complete concentration during performance. Every action has to fit together with up to one hundred other individuals exactly, and one has to enjoy that strict discipline and be convinced that the product is worth it. The possibility for emotional problems is high when such intensity is present, and the musical spirit can suffer damage when faced with uncaring people in authority.

My relations with the business management of the orchestra never convinced me that there was any interest in me or my colleagues as people with a life that included a family and other interests.

Musicians are sensitive, idealistic people generally. They never play poorly on purpose, and they never oppose a conductor unless to uphold what they feel to be musical reasons. Their loyalties are to the re-creation of music in a manner that will reflect the composer's style and intentions.

I suppose that a story of my own goof in a concert might be in order. Stravinsky was conducting one of his works that was not familiar to any of us. There was a horn solo of about four measures duration immediately following two or three time changes within less than a dozen measures. At rehearsal I had experienced no problems with the entrance and so was complacent and not aware of the possibility of miscounting the complicated rests through the time changes.

At the performance I started the solo either one beat too soon or one beat too late. I never did find out which, but one glance at Stravinsky left no doubt in my mind that I was not on the correct beat. He went into a little dance on the podium with elbows frantically waving in an effort to get me back on track, but of course I was unfamiliar with the piece and he had abandoned any semblance of a normal conducting pattern that would help me find the first beat of the measure. I buried my head behind the music stand and hung on until I ran out of notes. I then peeked out at him and was rewarded with a shrug of one shoulder as we continued on.

Being young and inexperienced, I thought I should offer an apology, so at the conclusion of the evening I made my way to his dressing room, knocked and was admitted. I apologized and had the following reply.

"Better horn players than you have done worse!"

I chose to regard that as a compliment, but I am still not sure whether or not that was what he intended.

Many musicians have never learned how to receive a compliment, and I believe that it is because we spend so much time striving for perfection. I can scarcely recall any time that I was satisfied with my performance. We have to be extremely self-critical in order to acquire and maintain standards demanded in our work. Often, after a concert, I would be going over the events of the evening to myself in order to plan how to do better next time, when someone would offer a compliment about an incidental solo that I had just decided was not my best work. Complete honesty at that point seems like overworking the "humble" bit, and also seems to be a message to the complimentor that he or she wouldn't know good music from bad! I finally learned to accept the other person's remarks graciously and gratefully.

Once a violinist I knew replied to a compliment by replying, *"It's just like shoveling coal."*

Well, I know that he was trying to be funny and relate the hard work that a musician does to other kinds of labor, but it started me thinking about a musician's contribution to humanity and how it compares to those who work at unskilled hard labor. Certainly what we do in our musical work requires great skill and concentration, but what, if any, is the value to society as a whole of our contribution? We can measure and evaluate the worth of the coal miner against the possibility of no coal for industry to use, and what alternative fuels would be used instead, etc. Those of us who have learned to enjoy symphonic music would feel bereft if there were no way to hear the great music composed for this huge musical instrument. The discussion is really about the importance of beauty in our lives. What are the effects on the human spirit of not experiencing beauty in painting, literature, philosophy, and music? Would man turn into a brutish, uncivilized creature if deprived of these finer experiences?

On the other hand, are the faithful attendees at concerts really uplifted by the music or are they thrilled by the evening out and the opportunity to rub elbows with the socially elite of the community? Probably both are part of the reason that people attend concerts with regularity.

I remarked earlier that the symphony orchestra is a kind of museum of sound that reproduces the creative work of well-known, and less well-known, composers. Music certainly has enhanced the lives of almost all human beings at some time, and so has value to mankind. I suppose that I became a musician primarily because music seemed to have more meaning to me than words. I have always found it more difficult to get meaning out of a lecture or sermon than almost any kind of music, in fact I rarely understand any of the words that singers either in a group or solo are singing. It doesn't matter to me what language an opera is in, I wouldn't understand anyway, but the music tells the story if well written.

What I have written in these pages, I did to amuse myself. Some of it is quite obviously inane. I have made no attempt to separate what is factual from what is the product of my own, admittedly weird, imagination, but I leave it up to the intelligence of anyone who may have been exposed to this writing, to use good common sense in order to tell what is likely and what is not.

I have been away from the professional side of music for a quarter-century now, but not a day goes by that I do not wish that it had been possible to remain in the music industry, because it was, without doubt, the place where I belonged. No other activity or job ever gave me the same sense of worthwhile accomplishment as did being a part of that marvelous musical organization known as the symphony orchestra.

Nevertheless, it has been pleasant to realize, as I awake each morning, that I will never again have to work my way through a Mahler or Bruchner symphony.

Epilogue

David Soter
1926 - 1994

Shortly before this book was completed, my friend and musical colleague, David Soter, died. We played in junior high school orchestra together, as well as in high school and for many years in a professional symphony orchestra. We shared after-concert dinners, complete with recaps of the evenings' events. David was a superb violinist who almost certainly could have made a success of a solo concert career if he had chosen to do so. He was as good a humorist and story teller as he was a musician, and often kept up the spirits of the first violins around him with some witticism or another, especially when the music business seemed most grim. Those of us who knew him and made music with him, were blessed beyond measure.

Drawing courtesy of
Greg Soter and Gail Jackson